THE

ITALIAN

KITCHEN

The

ITALIAN

KITCHEN

TRADITIONAL AND
CONTEMPORARY RECIPES
FOR PERFECT ITALIAN
CUISINE

This edition published in 2011

LOVE FOOD is an imprint of Parragon Books Ltd

Parragon
Queen Street House
4 Queen Street
Bath BA1 1HE, UK

ISBN: 978-1-4454-4450-5

Printed in China

Authors: Ingebrog Pils, Stefan Pallmer
Introduction: Linda Doeser
Photography: Martin Kurtenbach, Buenavista Studio

Notes for the Reader
This book uses both metric and imperial measurements. Follow the same units of measurement throughout; do not mix metric and imperial. All spoon measurements are level: teaspoons are assumed to be 5 ml, and tablespoons are assumed to be 15 ml. Unless otherwise stated, milk is assumed to be full fat, eggs and individual vegetables are medium, and pepper is freshly ground black pepper.

The times given are an approximate guide only. Preparation times differ according to the techniques used by different people and the cooking times may also vary from those given. Optional ingredients, variations or serving suggestions have not been included in the calculations.

Recipes using raw or very lightly cooked eggs should be avoided by infants, the elderly, pregnant women, convalescents and anyone suffering from an illness. Pregnant and breastfeeding women are advised to avoid eating peanuts and peanut products. Sufferers from nut allergies should be aware that some of the ready-made ingredients used in the recipes in this book may contain nuts. Always check the packaging before use

CONTENTS

INTRODUCTION

Italian food has conquered the world and there are few major cities that cannot boast a first class Italian restaurant. This unique cuisine delights with its fresh flavours, perfect combinations of ingredients, appetizing and often colourful appearance and its reputation for being one of the healthiest diets in the world.

A brief history of Italian cuisine

The story of Italian cooking is inextricably linked to the story of the country itself. Besides constructing roads, piping fresh water across the country and creating one of the greatest empires ever known, ancient Romans can also be credited with developing the first truly European cuisine. They were knowledgeable about food and farming and quick to exploit the natural riches of Italy – fish and seafood from the Mediterranean and Adriatic, game from the hillsides, and fresh fruit and vegetables transported daily from the countryside to the city. Farms raised goats, poultry and lamb, and the Romans were expert in the art of curing meat, particularly pork to produce superb ham.

When the Roman Empire collapsed, barbarian invasions in the north of Italy, destroyed much of its culture, including the cuisine. Conversely, the Saracen invasion in the south, especially in Sicily, brought new influences and new ingredients, such as rice, spinach and almonds. They may even have been responsible for the invention of spaghetti. Later, as Europe settled down, the Renaissance, which was a period of new economic, political, cultural and academic development, started to flourish and with it came a revival of the art of cooking. The aristocratic families of Naples, Florence and Milan delighted in good food and lavish banquets featuring soups, meat, game, poultry, fish, shellfish, vegetables, elaborate pies and tarts, a wide range of cheeses and all kinds of fruit. A thriving spice trade brought new flavours for chefs to experiment with.

Nowadays, it is strange to think of Italian cooking without tomatoes, but these, together with peppers, potatoes, maize and chocolate, did not appear on Italian tables until the eighteenth century when they were imported from the New World. American turkey and Yemeni coffee also began to appear in the Italian kitchen. It is curious and interesting that cookbooks at this time began to focus on domestic and regional cooking rather than the extravagant and cosmopolitan dishes prepared by chefs.

To talk about the history of Italian cuisine is somewhat misleading as the country was not unified until 1861. Before that, it consisted of a number of small states and principalities and this, too, has left its mark on Italian cooking. Even in these days of increased mobility, Italians are immensely loyal to their own province, hometown and even village – in cooking, just as much as in every other aspect of life.

Regional traditions

This is hardly surprising as using local produce lies at the very heart of Italian cooking. The south cooks with olive oil, whereas the north is ideal for dairy farming so butter is more traditional. Rice is the north's staple food, whereas the durum wheat grown in the warmer southern climate is used to make pasta. Each region has its own specialities and traditional recipes are passed down through the generations. The Pugliese are called 'leaf-eaters' because of the superb dishes made from their magnificent vegetable crops. Piedmont entices gastronomes from across the world with its incomparable white truffles. Lombardy is the home of many of Italy's best-known cheeses from mascarpone to Gorgonzola. Emilia-Romagna is rightly proud of its world-famous *prosciutto di Parma*, Parmesan cheese and balsamic vinegar. Tuscany, thought by some to produce the best olive oil in the world, is also known for the quality of its meat, poultry and game, not to mention its vast range of bean dishes that have caused Tuscans to be nicknamed 'bean-eaters'. Abruzzi is the home of the fiery hot *peperoncino* chilli, known locally as the 'little devil', while Naples in Campania claims to have invented dried pasta some six centuries ago. Sicily is famous for its sweetmeats and desserts.

SWITZERLAND

AUSTRIA

TRENTINO-
ALTO ADIGE

FRIULI-
VENEZIA
GIULIA

SLOVENIA

•Trento

LE D'AOSTA
Aosta

LOMBARDY

VENETO

Triest•

•Milan

Lake
Garda

Etsch

•Venice

•Turin

Po

PIEDMONT

EMILIA–ROMAGNA

LIGURIA
Genoa

•Bologna

Ligurian Sea

Arno

Florence•

Ancona
•

TUSCANY

THE MARCHE

Perugia•

UMBRIA

Adriatic Sea

Tiber

•L'Aquila

ABRUZZO

•Rome

MOLISE

LAZIO

Campobasso•

APULIA

CAMPANIA

Bari•

•Naples

•Potenza

BASILICATA

CALABRIA

Catanzaro•

Ionian Sea

•Palermo

SICILY

Seasonality and freshness

Italian cooking is undoubtedly shaped by the history of the country and the customs and produce of its regions, but two other, inextricably linked factors play an equally important role – seasonality and simplicity. The quintessential quality of all Italian recipes is the careful combination of a few complementary ingredients at the peak of perfection – fresh mozzarella, superbly ripe tomatoes and aromatic basil leaves drizzled with virgin olive oil is arguably one of the most delicious salads in the world or perfectly ripe strawberries sprinkled with sugar and aged balsamic vinegar then decorated with mint leaves makes a uniquely mouth-watering dessert.

Seasonality remains a priority – tomatoes, so integral to Italian cooking, must be at the sunshine peak of ripeness, fresh artichoke hearts can be found only in spring and if you want apricots other than straight off the tree in early summer, then they must be dried when freshly harvested. That is the true taste of Italy.

Italian food today

While regionalism is still acknowledged in Italian gastronomy – everyone knows that ossobucco is a Milanese speciality, saltimbocca comes from Rome and pizza Margherita was invented in Naples – the cuisine has become more integrated as have the people. The years following World War II saw massive migration from the poor rural communities of the south to the wealthier cities of the north. The migrants brought their culinary traditions with them, enriching those of their new homes, but rural communities were decimated and their culinary traditions began to disappear.

In addition, these years saw an increasing dominance of Anglo-American culture throughout Europe, and Italy was no exception. Fast food, convenience products and supermarkets all had their effect. However, campanilismo – a kind of proud parochialism – runs deep in Italy and the rural communities of the south, where farming rather than industry is the main occupation, held resolutely to their traditions. This, combined with an expanding tourist industry and the phenomenal spread of Italian restaurants in cities throughout the world, meant that the wonderful traditions of authentic traditional country fare were never completely lost.

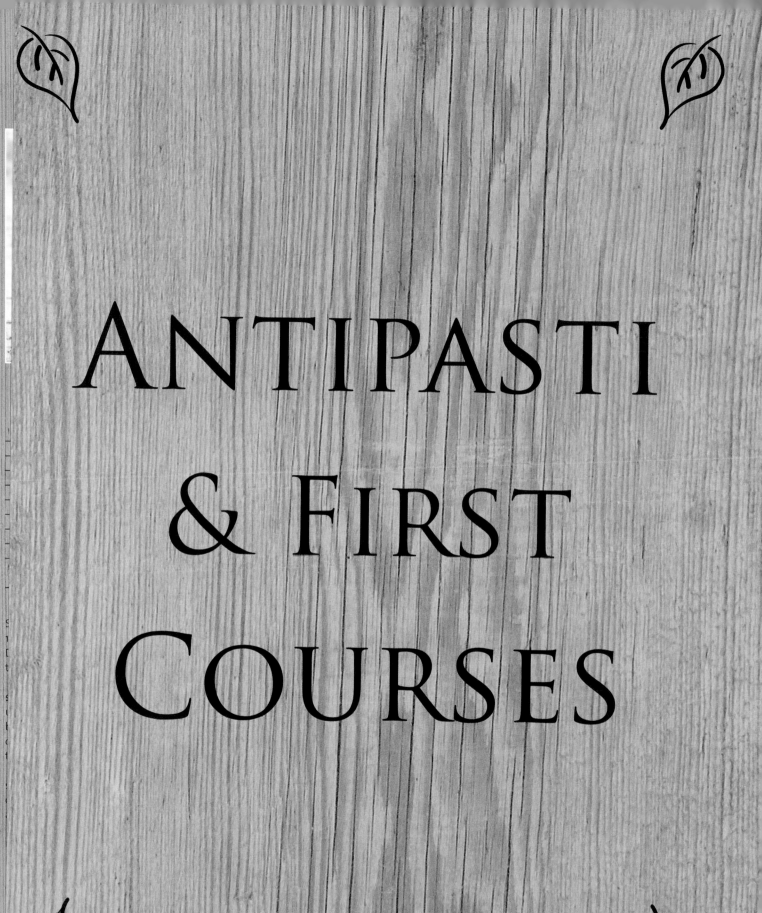

Antipasti & First Courses

Funghi sott'olio
Mushrooms Preserved in Oil

1 kg/2 lb 4 oz small mushrooms
(champignons, ceps, chanterelles,
honey mushrooms)

1 fresh red chilli

250 ml/9 fl oz olive oil

100 ml/3½ fl oz white balsamic vinegar

salt

1 small sprig oregano or rosemary

Clean the mushrooms and pat dry with paper towels. Cut the chilli in half, remove the core and cut the flesh into fine strips.

Heat 5 tablespoons of the olive oil in a large frying pan and brown the mushrooms on all sides until the liquid has evaporated.

Add the chilli to the pan and sauté briefly. Deglaze the pan with the vinegar, add salt, then transfer the mushrooms to a bowl. Add the herb and remaining olive oil. Cover and leave the mushrooms to marinate overnight.

Verdure sottaceto
Vegetables Pickled in Vinegar

For the marinade:

250 ml/9 fl oz dry white wine

200 ml/7 fl oz white wine vinegar

100 ml/3½ fl oz olive oil

1 piece lemon peel

5 sprigs parsley

1 celery stick, diced

1 sprig thyme

1 bay leaf

1 garlic clove

10 peppercorns

½ tsp salt

1 kg/2 lb 4 oz vegetables (carrots, celery,
green beans, asparagus, courgette,
cauliflower, peppers, leeks, onions)

1 tbsp sugar

juice of 1 lemon

salt

In a saucepan, bring to the boil 500 ml/ 18 fl oz of water and all the ingredients for the marinade. Simmer for 15 minutes.

Cut the vegetables into chunks of equal size. Fill another pan with salted water, add the sugar and lemon juice, and bring to the boil. Cook each vegetable in the water, separately, for 3 to 7 minutes depending on kind and size. Remove the vegetables, drain well and layer them inside a large bottling jar. Pour the boiling marinade over them and seal the jar. Marinate the vegetables in the refrigerator for at least two days.

Funghi sott'olio

Cipolle all'agrodolce
Pearl Onions in Balsamico

500 g/1 lb 2 oz pearl onions
1 garlic clove
2 sprigs thyme
2 bay leaves
2 cloves
5 black peppercorns
250 ml/9 fl oz red wine
125 ml/4 fl oz balsamic vinegar
1 tsp thyme honey
2 tbsp olive oil

Place the pearl onions and garlic in a saucepan. Add the thyme, bay leaves, cloves and peppercorns. Pour on the red wine and vinegar, and stir in the honey. Bring to the boil and simmer for approximately 25 minutes or until the pearl onions are soft.

Remove the pan from the stove and leave the onions to cool in the stock. Discard the thyme, bay leaves and cloves, then stir in the olive oil.

Fagioli all'agrodolce
Marinated White Beans

250 g/9 oz dried white beans
1 bay leaf
1 garlic clove
4 spring onions
1 tbsp lemon juice
3 tbsp white wine vinegar
5 tbsp olive oil
1 tbsp finely chopped parsley
50 g/1¾ oz grated Parmesan
salt and pepper

Soak the beans overnight in plenty of water. The next day, simmer the beans in the soaking water, adding the bay leaf and garlic to the pan. Bring to the boil, then skim off and cook on low heat until the beans are tender.

Remove the beans from the stove. Discard the garlic and bay leaf, then leave the beans to cool in the cooking liquid until lukewarm. Trim the spring onions and cut them into fine strips. Whisk the lemon juice, vinegar, oil, and salt and pepper to make a dressing.

Pour off the liquid from the beans and drain well. Combine the beans with the spring onions and dressing and leave to marinate for at least 15 minutes. Sprinkle with the parsley and grated Parmesan before serving.

Bay Leaves

The evergreen bay laurel tree, whose leaves were woven into victory crowns in ancient Roman times, originally came from the Middle East. Bay leaves were equally important for cooking in those days. Fresh or dried bay leaves flavoured soups, meat and fish dishes, sauces and pastas, lending them a tart and slightly bitter taste. But one should refrain from eating the leaves, and not only because of their intense flavour. The leathery leaf is no delicacy, and is therefore most often removed before serving. It is preferable not to use ground bay leaves because, like most spices, they lose much of their flavour once they are cut, leaving nothing but a bitter taste. For pickling vegetables, fresh bay leaves are far superior to dried ones, because they have a more intense flavour.

Fagioli all'agrodolce

Insalata caprese di bufala

Mozzarella

Nothing represents the colours of the Italian flag so delectably as fresh basil, tender mozzarella and aromatic tomatoes.

Mozzarella is a fresh, delicate white cheese with just a hint of sweetness. It is a *pasta filata*, or stretched-curd type of cheese (Italian: *filare*, to pull). As it is being made, the cheese curd is scalded and kneaded or stretched, then shaped into balls, plaits or other regionally typical configurations. It is most often sold fresh, packed in salt water. *Burrielli*, an exceptional delicacy, consists of little mozzarella balls that are stored in milk-filled clay amphoras. Mozzarella has experienced a similar culinary fate to that of Parmesan: both cheeses are famous in nearly every corner of the globe, yet it is mainly only cheap imitations of these Italian specialities that are sold. Authentic *mozzarella di bufala* is produced in the Aversa, Battipaglia, Capua, Eboli and Sessa Aurunca regions of Campania, and has carried the DOP (Protected Designation of Origin) certification mark since the 1990s. In order to claim DOP status, the cheese must be made from the milk of water buffalo cows that are raised on the open range and nourished with natural feed. Buffalo milk contains significantly more calcium, protein and fat than the milk of typical dairy cows.

Mozzarella di bufala is a speciality that comes at a price. That is why in many shops you will find the less expensive variety, *mozzarella fior di latte*, which is made from cow's milk and cannot come close to the flavour of the original. The two kinds of mozzarella differ not only in flavour: *mozzarella di bufala* contains over 50 per cent more fat, has 45 per cent less water than its cow's milk cousin and when sliced reveals a finely layered texture. It is best suited for fillings or for the famous *insalata caprese*, tomato slices with buffalo mozzarella and basil.

Basil

Basil has been cultivated for over 4,000 years. The ancient Greeks called the intensely aromatic plant 'the royal herb', and treasured not only its powerful fragrance, but also its healing properties. Basil originally came from Asia. Today there are at least sixty varieties of basil, the most familiar of which are small-leaf Greek basil, and sweet or Italian basil, also called *Basilico genovese*. Both of these have a distinctly different flavour than the Asian and African varieties. When used fresh, delicate green basil leaves from the Mediterranean regions have a slightly peppery, spicy-sweet flavour. These sensitive plants need a lot of sun and plentiful moisture. Liguria has nearly ideal climatic conditions for optimal cultivation, as does Piedmont. When using basil in cooking, it should not be cooked with the rest of the ingredients, but instead should be added at the end of the cooking process. Apropos, basil is a symbol of love in Italy.

Insalata caprese di bufala
Mozzarella with Tomatoes and Basil

500 g/1 lb 2 oz vine tomatoes, sliced

1 buffalo mozzarella, ca. 300 g/11 oz, sliced

1 bunch basil

4 tbsp olive oil

salt

freshly ground pepper

Arrange the tomato and mozzarella slices on four plates. Rinse the basil and shake it dry. Tear off the leaves and sprinkle them over the tomatoes and mozzarella slices.

Whisk the olive oil with salt and pepper and drizzle over the salad. Traditionally, *insalata caprese* is made without vinegar, but more and more often balsamic vinegar is added to the dressing.

Mozzarella in carozza
Breaded Mozzarella Sandwich

1 buffalo mozzarella, ca. 300 g/11 oz

8 thin slices white bread, with crusts removed

125 ml/4 fl oz milk

2 eggs

salt

freshly ground pepper

flour for breading

olive oil for frying

Cut the mozzarella into four slices slightly smaller than the bread. Arrange the cheese on four slices of bread, season with salt and pepper, then cover with the remaining bread and press down lightly. Pour the milk into a flat bowl, briefly turn each sandwich in it and press the bread firmly against the side of the bowl. Whisk the eggs in a deep dish. Turn the bread in the eggs to coat thoroughly, then coat in flour. Heat an ample amount of olive oil in a deep pan and fry the sandwiches on each side until golden brown. Serve very hot.

Only 'happy' water buffalo deliver milk for authentic mozzarella. The largest population of these animals lives in Campania on the Gulf of Naples.

To produce mozzarella, buffalo milk is first combined with rennet. The resulting cheese curd is cut into pieces and placed in a kettle.

The pieces of curd are then doused with hot water and pulled into strands by hand, using a wooden stick, until they become a doughy, elastic paste.

The uniform pieces are separated, then pulled into shape, kneaded and dunked again in hot whey until the desired consistency is achieved.

Stuffed Vegetables

Throughout the Mediterranean region, stuffed vegetables are very popular everyday fare. Fleshy vegetables with firm skins or rinds that can be thoroughly scooped out are best suited for this purpose. They should not be over-ripe, so that they hold their shape when filled and cooked.

The sky is the limit when it comes to the fillings. Raw vegetables such as tomatoes and cucumbers make excellent, flavourful 'packaging' for salads with mayonnaise. On the other hand, braised vegetables such as aubergine or courgette make delicious shells for mince or seasoned rice.

Stuffed vegetables are not only suitable as main dishes, but also as antipasti. When served as appetizers, they are often cut into bite-sized portions, and can be enjoyed hot or cold.

Pomodori ripieni di tonno
Stuffed Tomatoes

4 large, firm beef tomatoes
150 g/5 oz canned tuna in oil
2 eggs, hard boiled
1 small white onion, finely chopped
4 tbsp mayonnaise
1 tbsp finely chopped parsley
4 lettuce leaves
salt
freshly ground pepper

Wash the tomatoes and cut off the tops, including the stalks, for use as lids. Scoop out the core and seeds with a spoon.

Salt the insides of the tomatoes, place upside down in a sieve and drain.

Drain the tuna and flake with a fork. Peel and chop the eggs. Combine the onions, tuna and egg with the mayonnaise and parsley, then add salt and pepper to taste.

Put the filling in the tomatoes, set the tops back on and arrange the filled tomatoes on the lettuce leaves.

Pomodori ripieni di tonno

First remove the tops from the washed tomatoes and scoop out the core and seeds with a spoon. Only the firm flesh should remain.

Lightly salt the tomatoes to draw out some of the liquid. Place them upside down in a sieve and drain for 10 minutes.

For the stuffing, mix drained canned tuna with mayonnaise, finely chopped hard-boiled eggs and finely chopped onion and parsley. Season the mixture with salt and pepper.

Finally, stuff the hollow tomatoes with the tuna filling and place the tops over the stuffing to garnish. Arrange the stuffed vegetables on a plate and serve.

Funghi porcini ripieni
Stuffed Ceps

500 g/1 lb 2 oz ceps
100 ml/3½ fl oz olive oil,
plus extra for greasing
1 small white onion, finely chopped
1 garlic clove, minced
100 ml/3½ fl oz white wine
2 tbsp finely chopped parsley
50 g/1¾ oz grated Pecorino Romano
1 tbsp breadcrumbs
salt
freshly ground pepper

Grease a baking dish with olive oil. Clean the ceps. Remove the stalks from the caps and finely chop the stalks.

Heat half of the olive oil in a large frying pan and sauté the cep caps over low heat for about 5 minutes. Remove the mushroom caps from the pan and place them face down in the baking dish.

Sauté the onion, garlic and chopped cep stalks in the pan juices for 5 minutes, stirring continuously. Deglaze with the wine, then stir in the parsley. Season with salt and pepper, and simmer for another 5 minutes.

Use the mixture to stuff the mushroom caps. Mix the Pecorino Romano and breadcrumbs and sprinkle over the stuffed caps. Drizzle with the remaining olive oil and brown for a few minutes under the grill.

Cipolle ripiene
Stuffed Onions

4 large onions
50 g/1¾ oz prosciutto,
cut into fine strips
1 tbsp finely chopped sage
1 tbsp finely chopped oregano
200 g/7 oz fresh goat's cheese
1 egg, beaten
125 ml/4 fl oz white wine
60 g/2 oz grated Parmesan
salt
freshly ground pepper

Preheat the oven to 175°C/350°F/gas mark 4. Peel the onions. Bring a saucepan of salted water to the boil and cook the onions for 10 to 15 minutes. Then refresh them in cold water, cool a little longer, and cut off the top third for use as a lid. Carefully scoop out the onions with a spoon, leaving a shell about 1 cm/½ inch thick. Finely dice the scooped-out flesh.

Combine the diced onion, ham and herbs with the cheese and egg. Season with salt and pepper. Fill the onion shells with this mixture and top them with the onion lids.

Place the stuffed onions close together in a baking dish and pour the wine over them. Cover the dish with aluminium foil and bake for 30 to 40 minutes. Sprinkle the stuffed onions with the grated Parmesan before serving.

Cipolle ripiene

Pizza

There is probably no other dish that is as internationally synonymous with Italian cuisine as the *pizza*, although Italians principally understand it to mean Neapolitan pizza. This is all the more remarkable since pizza is the offspring of peasants' kitchens. Born of necessity, it was the means to concoct a flavourful, satisfying meal from a few very simple ingredients.

The first written pizza recipe dates back to 1858, but Neapolitans were already familiar with it at the beginning of the eighteenth century. Pizza dough with tomatoes was first documented in Naples at the end of the seventeenth century. Pizza's triumphal journey around the globe did not start in Naples, but rather in far away New York City. In 1905, Signore Lombardi opened the first pizzeria in New York's Little Italy neighbourhood. American pizzas, unlike those from pizza's hometown of Naples, were lavishly decked out with a variety of ingredients and soon became a smash hit. Indeed, pizza is one of the Americans' favourite foods: 40 hectares of pizza is consumed every day in the United States!

Basic Pizza Dough

40 g/1½ oz compressed fresh yeast or 2 sachets easy-blend dried yeast
½ tsp sugar
400 g/14 oz flour, plus extra for dusting
1 tsp salt
3 tbsp olive oil

Crumble the yeast into a small bowl and sprinkle with the sugar. Add 125 ml/4 fl oz lukewarm water, then stir to dissolve the yeast and sugar. Cover with a clean tea towel and prove in a warm spot for 30 minutes. Sift the flour into a large bowl. Make a hollow in the centre and pour the yeast mixture, salt, olive oil and 5–7 tablespoons of water into it. Knead everything into a smooth, silky dough, then shape it into a ball. Dust the ball with a little flour, cover and set aside in a warm place to rise for an additional hour, or until doubled in volume.

Pizzette

Pizzette
Small Pizzas

40 g/1½ oz compressed fresh yeast or 2 sachets easy-blend dried yeast
½ tsp sugar
400 g/14 oz flour, plus extra for dusting
1 tsp salt
60 ml/2 fl oz olive oil, plus extra for greasing
500 g/1 lb 2 oz tomatoes
1 radicchio
100 g/3½ oz bacon, cut into strips
50 g/1¾ oz pine kernels

Crumble the yeast into a small bowl and sprinkle with the sugar. Add 125 ml/4 fl oz lukewarm water, then stir to dissolve the yeast and sugar. Cover with a clean tea towel and prove in a warm spot for 30 minutes. Sift the flour into a large bowl. Make a hollow in the centre and pour the yeast mixture, salt, 3 tablespoons of olive oil and 5–7 tablespoons of water into it. Knead everything into a smooth, silky dough, then shape it into a ball. Dust the ball with a little flour, cover and set aside in a warm place to rise for about 1 hour or until doubled in volume.

Grease two baking sheets with olive oil and preheat the oven to 200°C/390°F/gas mark 6. Peel and quarter the tomatoes, remove the seeds, and cut into small dice. Trim the radicchio and break it into bite-sized pieces.

Divide the dough into 12 equal pieces. Form each into a ball, flatten and place the rounds on the baking sheets. Top with the diced tomato and bacon and drizzle on the remaining oil. Bake for 15 minutes, then sprinkle the radicchio and pine kernels over the *pizzette* and bake for another 5 minutes.

Pizza di patate
Apulian Potato Pizza

750 g/1 lb 10 oz potatoes
1 tsp salt
3 tbsp flour
70 ml/2½ fl oz olive oil, plus extra for greasing
400 g/14 oz canned peeled tomatoes
100 g/3½ oz black olives
12 anchovies in oil
150 g/5 oz feta cheese, diced
1 onion, cut into rings
2 garlic cloves, finely chopped
½ tsp rosemary
½ tsp dried oregano
freshly ground pepper

Bring a saucepan of salted water to the bo and cook the potatoes. Drain, rinse them cold water, peel, and put through a potat press while still hot. Stir in the salt, flour ar 2 tablespoons of the olive oil and leave th mixture to cool.

Grease a springform cake tin (28 cm 11 inches in diameter) with olive oil and pr heat the oven to 220°C/430°F/gas mark Drain the tomatoes and cut them into sma pieces. Press the potato dough into the pa creating a rim. Spread the tomatoes, olive anchovies, feta cheese, onion and garlic c the dough. Sprinkle with rosemary, oregar and pepper, then bake for approximate 30 minutes.

Pizza Margherita

1 pizza dough
(see recipe on page 28)
75 ml/2½ fl oz olive oil,
plus extra for greasing
2 small onions, diced
400 g/14 oz canned diced tomatoes
50 g/1¾ oz canned tomato sauce
1 tsp oregano
400 g/14 oz mozzarella
salt and pepper
flour for dusting
basil leaves to garnish

Heat 4 tablespoons of the olive oil and sauté the onions until translucent. Add both kinds of tomatoes and the oregano, and season with salt and pepper. Cook the sauce for about 30 minutes on medium heat.

Preheat the oven to 225°C/435°F/gas mark 7 and grease four round pizza pans with olive oil. Divide the dough into four equal portions and roll them into circles on a floured surface. Place the circles of dough on the pizza pans.

Thinly slice the mozzarella. Brush the dough with the tomato sauce, cover with mozzarella slices, and drizzle on the remaining olive oil. Bake for about 20 minutes, then garnish with basil leaves and serve immediately.

Pizza alla marinara
Mariner's Pizza

1 pizza dough
(see recipe on page 28)
800 g/1 lb 12 oz canned diced tomatoes
3–4 garlic cloves, finely chopped
1 tbsp oregano
50 g/1¾ oz capers
100 g/3½ oz black olives
200 g/7 oz Bel Paese cheese, grated
3 tbsp olive oil, plus extra for greasing
flour for dusting
salt
freshly ground pepper

Preheat the oven to 225°C/435°F/gas mark 7 and grease four round pizza pans with olive oil. Divide the dough into four equal portions and roll them into circles on a floured surface. Place the circles of dough on the pizza pans.

Distribute the tomatoes on the dough. Season with the garlic, oregano, salt and pepper. Scatter on the capers and olives and sprinkle with the grated cheese. Drizzle on the olive oil, then bake the pizzas for about 20 minutes.

Pizza quattro stagioni
Four Seasons Pizza

1 pizza dough
(see recipe on page 28)
1 tbsp butter
200 g/7 oz mushrooms, sliced
4 tomatoes
200 g/7 oz cooked ham
200 g/7 oz mozzarella
4 artichoke hearts in oil
16 black olives
1 tsp oregano
4 tbsp olive oil, plus extra for greasing
flour for dusting
salt and pepper

Preheat the oven to 225°C/435°F/gas mark 7 and grease four round pizza pans with olive oil. Heat the butter and sauté the mushrooms for 10 minutes. Peel and quarter the tomatoes, remove the seeds, and cut into small dice. Cut the ham into small pieces. Thinly slice the mozzarella. Quarter the artichoke hearts.

Divide the dough into four equal portions and roll them into circles on a floured surface. Place the circles of dough on the pizza pans.

Distribute the tomatoes and mozzarella evenly on the pizzas. Cover one quarter of each of the pizzas with one of the following toppings: mushrooms, ham, artichokes and olives. Season with the oregano, salt and pepper and drizzle with the olive oil. Bake for about 20 minutes.

Favourite Salads

Insalata di arance
Orange Salad

4 oranges
1 red onion
2 tbsp finely chopped parsley
4 tbsp olive oil
salt
freshly ground pepper

Peel the oranges and remove the pith, then slice in rounds. Lay them out in a fan pattern on a plate. Peel and halve the onion, and thinly slice one half. Finely chop the other and combine with the parsley.

Sprinkle the sliced and chopped onions over the orange slices, season with a little salt and pepper, and drizzle olive oil over the salad. Cover with clingfilm and marinate for 1 hour in the refrigerator. Remove from the refrigerator 5 minutes before serving.

Insalata di tonno e fagioli
Bean Salad with Tuna

400 g/14 oz white beans, cooked
4 spring onions, finely chopped
1 fresh red chilli, finely chopped
2 celery sticks, finely diced
2 tbsp lemon juice
6 tbsp olive oil
170 g/6 oz canned tuna in oil
1 tbsp finely chopped parsley
salt
freshly ground pepper

Mix together the cooked beans, spring onions, chilli and celery. Whisk together the lemon juice and olive oil to make a dressing, season with salt and pepper, and pour it over the salad. Set aside to marinate for 15 minutes.

Drain the tuna fish and break into bite-sized chunks. Stir the tuna and parsley into the bean salad.

Olio e sale alla barese
Tomato Salad with Cucumber, Onion and Bread

1 small cucumber, peeled
2 beef tomatoes
1 white onion
4 tbsp olive oil
2 tbsp white wine vinegar
2 slices of white country bread
salt
freshly ground pepper

Slice the cucumber and tomatoes and place them in a salad bowl. Slice the onion into fine rings, then toss them with the cucumber and tomatoes.

Whisk together the olive oil and vinegar, season with salt and pepper, and pour over the salad. Marinate for 20 minutes.

Toast the bread slices on both sides under a grill or in the oven until golden brown, then cut into bite-sized pieces. Toss them into the salad and serve immediately.

Insalata di carciofi
Artichoke Salad

8 small purple artichokes
3 tbsp lemon juice
250 ml/9 fl oz white wine
½ tsp salt, plus extra to season
100 ml/3½ fl oz olive oil
2 garlic cloves, finely chopped
1 small red onion, finely chopped
2 tbsp tarragon vinegar
6 basil leaves
freshly ground pepper

Remove the hard outer leaves from the artichokes and cut away the upper half of the tender inner leaves. Shorten the stalks to 5 cm and peel them. Immediately place the artichokes in a saucepan with water and the lemon juice.

Add the white wine, salt and 2 tablespoons of the olive oil to the pan and bring to the boil. Cover and simmer on medium heat for 20 to 25 minutes. Then take the artichokes out of the water, cool slightly, then cut them in half lengthways.

Stir the garlic and onion with 2 tablespoons of the artichoke cooking water, the tarragon vinegar, and salt and pepper to taste. Mix in the remaining olive oil. Cut the basil leaves into fine strips. Lay the artichoke halves face up in a bowl, pour the dressing over them and sprinkle the basil on top. Serve while moderately hot.

Radicchio alla vicentina
Radicchio Salad

400 g/14 oz radicchio di Chioggia
100 g/3½ oz pancetta
1 tbsp olive oil
2 tbsp balsamic vinegar
salt
freshly ground pepper

Trim and wash the radicchio, then spin it dry. Tear the leaves into bite-sized pieces and arrange them on four plates. Finely dice the pancetta.

Heat the olive oil in a frying pan and fry the pancetta until crisp. Deglaze with the vinegar and season with salt and pepper. Pour the pancetta and pan juices over the radicchio and serve immediately.

Panzanella
Bread Salad

400 g/14 oz day-old
Tuscan country bread

1 small cucumber

2 small white onions

100 ml/3½ fl oz olive oil

2–3 tbsp red wine vinegar

500 g/1 lb 2 oz tomatoes, sliced

1 handful rocket

salt

freshly ground pepper

Cut the bread into slices about 2 cm/¾ inch thick and soak them in a bowl of cold water for no more than 10 minutes.

Peel the cucumber, cut it in half lengthways, and deseed. Thinly slice the cucumber halves. Slice the onions into fine rings. Thoroughly squeeze the water from the bread slices and tear into bite-sized pieces.

Heat half the olive oil in a non-stick frying pan and sauté the bread, turning it constantly. Remove from the heat and leave to cool.

Whisk together the remaining olive oil, the vinegar, salt and pepper. In a larger bowl, combine the cucumbers, tomatoes, onions, toast and dressing.

Wash the rocket, removing any wilted leaves or coarse stalks, and pat it dry. Line four bowls with the rocket and arrange the bread salad on it. In the original version, bread salad was covered and left to marinate in a cool place for several hours. Nowadays, it is usually served immediately so that the toast remains crisp.

Asparagi all'olio e aceto balsamico
Asparagus Salad
with Balsamic Vinegar

400 g/14 oz each: green asparagus,
white asparagus

75 ml/2½ fl oz olive oil

2 tbsp balsamic vinegar

salt

freshly ground pepper

parsley leaves to garnish

Wash and trim the asparagus. Lightly peel the white asparagus and remove the woody ends from both kinds. Cut all the asparagus stalks to the same length, bundle them in portions and place in a deep, narrow saucepan. Fill the pan two-thirds full with cold water, add a little salt, cover the pan and bring to the boil. Cook until the asparagus is tender yet still crisp.

Remove the asparagus from the water and drain well. Whisk together the olive oil, vinegar, salt and pepper to make a dressing. Lay the asparagus on a serving plate, pour the dressing over it and garnish with parsley. Serve while moderately hot.

Rucola

Rucola is an annual wild herb with long, dark green leaves that is known by many names in English: rocket, Italian cress, arugula or rucola. The variety with delicate leaves is a familiar salad ingredient, whereas the broad-leaved version is mainly used to produce oil. The more mature types of rocket taste slightly sour and a little peppery. Most cultivated types of rocket that are available today have a predominantly nutty, mild flavour. Although it looks robust at first glance, rocket is very delicate and wilts easily. It is most often used in combination with other salad leaves, often with fruit. Rocket with bresaola or prosciutto and Parmesan is a very popular appetizer, but rocket is being used more and more on pizzas, or finely cut and mixed into pasta dishes.

Insalata con rucola e parmigiano
Rocket and Parmesan Salad

2 handfuls rocket

1 small fennel bulb

75 ml/2½ fl oz olive oil

2 tbsp balsamic vinegar

100 g/3½ oz Parmesan

50 g/1¾ oz pine kernels

salt

freshly ground pepper

Wash the rocket, removing any wilted leaves or coarse stalks, and pat it dry. Divide the leaves among four plates. Halve the fennel bulb, slice it finely and spread some over the rocket on each plate.

Whisk together the olive oil, balsamic vinegar, salt and pepper and drizzle over the salad. Top the salad with shaved Parmesan. Dry-roast the pine kernels in an ungreased frying pan until golden brown, then sprinkle over each serving of salad.

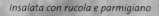
Insalata con rucola e parmigiano

P
s
4
a
1
a
1
a
th
th

b
re
fo
to
o
P
h
p

Favourite Fish Dishes

Trotelle ai funghi porcini
Trout Fillets with Ceps

8 trout fillets

1 tbsp chopped tarragon

500 ml/18 fl oz white wine

500 g/1 lb 2 oz ceps

100 g/3½ oz butter

1 small onion, finely chopped

1 tbsp chopped thyme

salt

freshly ground pepper

Wash the trout fillets, pat them dry, and ru
with salt and pepper. Place the fish in a bow
sprinkle with the tarragon and pour 125 ml
4 fl oz wine over them. Cover the bowl an
marinate for 30 minutes.

Meanwhile, wipe the ceps with a dam
cloth, trim the stalks and cut them into 1-cm
⅓-inch thick slices. Heat half of the butte
and sauté the onion until translucent. Ad
the mushrooms and sauté while stirring unt
the liquid has evaporated. Pour in the rest c
the wine and season with salt, pepper and th
thyme. Simmer on low heat for 10 minutes.

Melt the rest of the butter in a large, nor
stick frying pan. Remove the trout fillets fror
the marinade, pat them dry and sauté in hc
butter for 3 minutes on each side. Then pou
in the marinade and bring it to the boil. Serv
the mushrooms with the fish.

Trote affogate
Trout in White Wine

4 fresh brook trout; ready to cook

75 ml/2½ fl oz olive oil

1 white onion, finely chopped

2 garlic cloves, finely chopped

1 tbsp finely chopped parsley

125 ml/4 fl oz white wine

salt

freshly ground pepper

flour

Wash the trout, pat them dry, and seaso
with salt and pepper. Coat in flour and tap o
the excess.

Heat the oil in a large frying pan and plac
the trout in the pan. Add the onion, garlic an
parsley. Fry the trout for 4 minutes on eac
side on medium heat.

Pour in the wine and cook the trout on lo
heat for an additional 10 minutes. Pour th
cooking juices over the fish before serving.

Brodetto friulano
Friulian Fish Stew

1 kg/2 lb 4 oz mixed freshwater fish
(for example, perch, eel, tench or perch),
ready to cook

1 white onion

2 garlic cloves

2 carrots

2 celery sticks

250 g/9 oz tomatoes

2 tbsp olive oil

500 ml/18 fl oz fish stock

2 bay leaves

1 tbsp balsamic vinegar

4 slices white bread

salt

freshly ground pepper

Wash the fish, pat it dry and cut into bite-sized pieces. Season with salt and pepper. Finely dice the onion and garlic. Cut the carrots and celery into fine dice. Peel and quarter the tomatoes, remove the core, and cut into fine dice.

Heat the olive oil in a saucepan and sauté the onions and garlic. Add the carrots and celery, browning lightly. Mix in the tomatoes, pour in the fish stock and add the bay leaves. Simmer together for 10 minutes.

Add the fish to the stew and cook on low heat for about 10 minutes. Remove the bay leaves and season the stew with salt, pepper and the balsamic vinegar. Toast the white bread and place each slice in a deep bowl. Ladle the fish stew over the toast and serve immediately.

Triglie di fango al pesto
Red Mullet with Parsley Pesto

4 red mullet or red snapper,
300 g/11 oz each, ready to cook
juice of 1 lemon
60 g/2 oz pine kernels
2 garlic cloves, chopped
1 tsp salt, plus extra to season
2 bunches parsley, finely chopped
150 ml/5 fl oz olive oil
2 tbsp grated Parmesan
freshly ground pepper
flour for coating
lemon wedges to garnish

Wash the fish, pat it dry and sprinkle with the lemon juice. Season the fish inside and out with salt and pepper.

Dry-roast the pine kernels in an ungreased frying pan until golden brown. Remove from the heat and leave to cool.

Crush the garlic and salt with a mortar and pestle. Add the pine kernels and parsley, and crush into a paste. Gradually work in 7 tablespoons of the olive oil. Mix in the Parmesan last, adding a little water if needed.

Heat the remaining oil in a large frying pan. Coat the fish in flour and shake off the excess, then fry the fish in the hot oil for 4 to 5 minutes per side. Remove them from the pan and place on four heated plates. Serve topped with the parsley pesto and garnished with lemon wedges.

Sogliola ai carciofi
Sole with Artichokes

8 small purple artichokes
juice of 1 lemon
125 ml/4 fl oz olive oil
4 garlic cloves, finely sliced
250 ml/9 fl oz dry white wine
400 ml/14 fl oz stock
800 g/1 lb 12 oz fillet of sole
salt
freshly ground pepper
flour for coating
1 tbsp finely chopped parsley

Clean the artichokes, then shorten the stalks to about 4 cm/1½ inches and peel them. Remove the tough outer leaves and trim the hard thorns from the remaining leaves. Mix the lemon juice and some water in a bowl. Slice the artichokes lengthways and immediately put them in the lemon water. Marinate for a short time, then pour off the liquid and pat the artichokes dry.

Heat 6 tablespoons of the olive oil in a large frying pan and sauté the artichokes. Add the garlic and sauté until golden brown. Deglaze with the wine, pour in the stock, and add salt and pepper. Simmer for 20 to 25 minutes, then remove from the stovetop.

Season the fish fillets with salt and pepper, coat in flour and shake off the excess. Heat the remaining oil and fry the fish on both sides. Serve the fish over the artichokes, sprinkled with the chopped parsley.

Branzino ripieno
Stuffed Sea Bass

10 g/⅓ oz dried ceps
100 g/3½ oz cooked prawns, shelled
1 tbsp chopped thyme
1 egg
1–2 tbsp breadcrumbs
1 sea bass, ca. 1.4 kg/3 lb, ready to cook
1 onion, cut into thin rings
2 tbsp butter
250 ml/9 fl oz white wine
oil for greasing
freshly grated nutmeg
salt
freshly ground pepper

Soak the ceps in 150 ml/5 fl oz hot water for 15 minutes, then pour the liquid through a fine sieve and reserve it for later. Drain and finely chop the ceps.

Preheat the oven to 175°C/350°F/gas mark 4 and grease a baking dish with oil. Finely chop the prawns and mix with the mushrooms, thyme, egg and breadcrumbs. Season with nutmeg. Wash the fish, pat it dry, and rub inside and out with salt.

Stuff the fish with the mushroom-prawn mixture and close the opening with wooden skewers. Place the onion rings in the base of the baking dish, then lay the fish on them. Put little pats of butter on top of the fish. Pour in the reserved soaking water and half the wine. Bake the fish for about 45 minutes, gradually adding the rest of the wine during that time.

Transfer the fish to a heated platter. Pour off the cooking juices, season with salt and pepper, and serve with the fish.

Branzino alla pugliese
Braised Sea Bass with Courgette

1 sea bass, ca. 1 kg/2 lb 4 oz, ready to cook
2 firm potatoes
2 large courgettes
2 garlic cloves, finely chopped
½ tsp salt, plus extra to season
150 ml/5 fl oz olive oil
2 tbsp finely chopped parsley
250 ml/9 fl oz white wine
freshly ground pepper

Preheat the oven to 180°C/355°F/gas mark 4. Wash the fish, pat it dry, and season inside and out with salt and pepper. Peel and thinly slice the potatoes. Wash the courgettes and finely slice them lengthways.

Crush the garlic and salt with a mortar and pestle, then stir them into the oil and mix with the parsley. Pour half of the oil mixture into a baking dish and place the courgette slices in it. Season with pepper. Lay the fish on the courgette. Arrange the potato slices so they fan out over the fish and drizzle the rest of the oil mixture over them.

Bake the fish for 15 minutes. Then pour in the white wine and braise for an additional 30 minutes. Serve in the baking dish.

Coda di rospo al rosmarino
Monkfish with Rosemary

800 g/1 lb 12 oz monkfish
(without the head)
150 ml/5 fl oz olive oil
3 sprigs rosemary
3 garlic cloves, peeled
salt
freshly ground pepper

Detach the monkfish fillets from the backbone, wash them, pat dry, and season with salt and pepper.

Heat the olive oil slightly in a deep frying pan. Add the rosemary and garlic and sauté for several minutes. Then remove the garlic and put the fish in the pan. Fry on medium heat for 3 minutes on each side. Serve the monkfish over a vegetable risotto.

Involtini di pesce spada
Swordfish Roulades

4 long, thin swordfish slices,
ca. 200 g/7 oz each
5 tbsp olive oil
1 small onion, finely chopped
1 garlic clove, finely chopped
2 tbsp finely chopped parsley
2 tbsp grated Pecorino Romano
2 tbsp breadcrumbs
125 ml/4 fl oz white wine
1 tbsp chopped thyme
lemon juice for sprinkling
salt
freshly ground pepper
cayenne pepper
flour for coating

Wash the fish, pat it dry and sprinkle with lemon juice. Heat 2 tablespoons of olive oil in a frying pan and sauté the onion and garlic. Mix in the parsley, then remove from the stove and leave to cool.

Stir the Pecorino Romano and breadcrumbs into the onion mixture. Season with salt and cayenne pepper. Spread the mixture on the fish slices, roll them up and secure with wooden skewers.

Heat the remaining olive oil in a separate pan. Coat the fish roulades in flour and fry on all sides for 10 to 12 minutes on low heat. Then remove from the pan and keep warm. Deglaze the pan drippings with wine and season the sauce with thyme, salt and pepper. Serve the roulades with the sauce.

Involtini di mullo alle erbe
Red Mullet with Herb Stuffing

20 red mullet or
red snapper fillets (with skin)
juice of 1 lemon
2 garlic cloves
1 small onion
3 tbsp olive oil, plus extra for greasing
2 tbsp finely chopped parsley
8 sage leaves, finely chopped
10 thin slices raw ham, halved
125 ml/4 fl oz white wine
4 tbsp breadcrumbs
salt
freshly ground pepper

Preheat the oven to 200°C/390°F/gas mark 6 and grease a baking dish with olive oil. Wash the fish fillets, pat them dry, and season with salt and pepper. Lay them on a platter and sprinkle with the lemon juice.

Mince the garlic and onion. Heat 1 tablespoon of the olive oil in a frying pan and sauté the garlic, onion and herbs. Remove from the stove and leave to cool slightly.

Place the fillets skin-side down on a work surface. Spread some of the herb and onion mixture over each one, then lay a half slice of ham on top. Roll up the fillets and secure with wooden skewers.

Place the roulades in the baking dish side by side. Bring the wine to the boil, then pour it over the fish. Sprinkle breadcrumbs over the top and drizzle on the remaining oil. Bake for 15 minutes.

Coda di rospo al rosmarino

Involtini di mullo alle erbe

Tonno fresco al forno
Baked Tuna

700 g/1 lb 9 oz tuna steak
2 tbsp lemon juice
2 bay leaves
several sprigs fennel greens
4 shallots, diced
100 ml/3½ fl oz olive oil
250 ml/9 fl oz dry white wine
salt
freshly ground pepper
flour for coating

Preheat the oven to 175°C/350°F/gas mark 4. Wash the tuna, pat it dry, and season with salt and pepper. Sprinkle it with the lemon juice, then coat in flour and tap off the excess.

Place the fish in a baking dish and lay the bay leaves and fennel greens on top of it. Scatter the diced shallots around the fish. Drizzle with the olive oil and pour in the white wine.

Cover the dish with aluminium foil. Bake the tuna for 40 minutes, removing the aluminium foil for the last 10 minutes. Cut the fish into four pieces of equal size and serve with the shallots.

Tonno all'alloro
Tuna with Bay Leaves

4 fresh tuna steaks, 250 g/9 oz each
120 ml olive oil
juice of 1 lemon
12 bay leaves
salt
freshly ground pepper

Wash the tuna and pat it dry with paper towels. Whisk together 5 tablespoons of the olive oil, the lemon juice, and salt and pepper. Brush the tuna steaks with the dressing.

Crush the bay leaves several times to release their essential oils. Stack the tuna steaks on top of one another with the bay leaves in between them. Wrap the fish in clingfilm and chill in the refrigerator for about 3 hours.

Heat the remaining olive oil in a large frying pan. Remove the clingfilm and bay leaves from the fish, then fry the fish steaks in oil for about 5 minutes per side.

Coda di rospo al vino bianco
Monkfish in White Wine Sauce

8 small monkfish fillets
5 tbsp olive oil
1 onion, finely chopped
2 garlic cloves, finely chopped
2 celery sticks, diced
2 tbsp finely chopped parsley
250 ml/9 fl oz white wine
salt
freshly ground pepper
flour for dusting

Wash the fish fillets and pat dry. Preheat the oven to 200°C/390°F/gas mark 6.

Heat 2 tablespoons of the olive oil in a frying pan and sauté the onions, garlic and celery. Stir in the parsley and then transfer the vegetables to a baking dish.

Season the fish fillets with salt and pepper, then dust lightly with flour. Heat the remaining oil in a frying pan and fry the fish briefly on both sides. Then remove the fish from pan and place it on the vegetables. Pour the pan juices over it and add the wine. Bake for 10 to 15 minutes until done.

Tonno fresco al forno

Filetti di sogliola al cartoccio
Fillet of Sole in Baking Paper

4 large sole fillets
50 g/1¾ oz stoned black olives
1 tbsp finely chopped oregano
2 tbsp finely chopped parsley
3 tbsp olive oil, plus extra for greasing
2 tbsp lemon juice
salt
freshly ground pepper

Preheat the oven to 180°C/355°F/gas mark 4. Wash the fish fillets and pat them dry. Finely chop the olives and combine them with the oregano, parsley and olive oil.

Grease four sheets of baking paper with olive oil and lay one sole fillet on each. Season with salt, pepper and lemon juice, then spread the olive-herb mixture over the fish. Enclose the fish fillets in baking paper, being sure to seal the packets tightly. Bake the fish for 6 to 7 minutes. Serve in the baking paper.

Cooking in Baking Paper

From very early in history, our ancestors began to wrap vegetables, meat, fish and poultry in a protective covering of leaves or clay and then cook them gently and slowly.

Wrapping food in something serves two functions. First, it protects the flavouring on the inside and prevents the food drying out. The meal stews in its own juices and retains valuable nutrients, its unique flavour and original shape. Also, unhealthy by-products of roasting are prevented from developing by this method. This gentle means of cooking is especially well suited to fish.

Baking paper has two qualities that are ideal for cooking: it does not get too hot, and it 'breathes', which promotes the unfolding of flavours during the cooking process. Baking paper was developed specially for this gentle cooking method, but simple greaseproof paper can also be used, in layers of three sheets and well oiled, because it must not become saturated. Caution is advised: the oven temperature must not exceed 190°C (375°F) or the paper can catch fire.

Shrimps, Prawns and Scampi

Whether it is tiny bay shrimp, prawns or scampi, these delicious creatures taste best when they are freshly caught and boiled, grilled or baked right in their shells. Diners encountering prawns for the first time may wonder how best to handle these armoured delicacies. The easiest way is to use one's fingers. Even in the best restaurants, this method is entirely customary.

Since the head is simply unpalatable, start by removing it and setting it aside. Then bend the armored shell outwards along the stomach and detach the meat from the shell. If the dark vein along the back of the prawn is still visible, it can be removed with the point of a knife. If no extra plates have been provided, just slide the discarded parts to the edge of the plate.

Now nothing stands in the way of delicious eating. The shelled prawns are taken in the hand, dipped into a sauce or dip and eaten. The little bowl of lemon water that is served with them in many Italian restaurants is intended for washing your hands after the meal.

Pick up the prawn with your hand, remove the head and set it aside. It is not edible.

With your fingers, remove the shell from the stomach outwards.

Cut along the back of the prawn with a sharp knife to de-vein.

Dip the shelled prawn in the sauce with your fingers. Enjoy!

Gamberoni arrabbiati
Prawns Arrabbiata

500 g/1 lb 2 oz raw prawns
145 ml/5 fl oz olive oil
1 fresh red chilli, finely chopped
2 tbsp lemon juice
2½ tbsp Italian brandy
2 garlic cloves
500 g/1 lb 2 oz tomatoes, diced
125 ml/4 fl oz white wine
salt
freshly ground pepper
several small basil leaves

Prepare the prawns as described above. Stir 6 tablespoons of the olive oil together with the chilli, lemon juice and brandy. Peel the garlic and press it into the seasoned oil. Marinate the prawns in it for 1 hour.

Heat the remaining olive oil in a frying pan and sauté the prawns for about 3 minutes per side. Remove them from the pan and keep warm. Cook the tomatoes in the pan oil and deglaze with the wine. Put the prawns back in the pan, then season the sauce with salt and pepper. Serve garnished with basil leaves.

Gamberoni alla griglia
Chargrilled Prawns

20 raw prawns
3 large garlic cloves
100 ml/3½ fl oz olive oil
⅛ teaspoon cayenne pepper
1 tsp dried oregano
1 lemon

Soak four wooden skewers in water. Wash the prawns and pat them dry. Peel the garlic and press it into the olive oil. Stir in the cayenne pepper and oregano. Place the prawns in a bowl and pour the garlic oil over them. Cover the bowl and marinate the prawns in the refrigerator for 4 hours, turning once. Place five prawns on each of the wooden skewers, and barbecue or grill for 5 minutes per side. Cut the lemon into wedges and serve with the prawns.

Crayfish

Italian rivers and brooks were once filled with crayfish, which were popular, everyday fare. However, their populations decreased drastically as water pollution became increasingly prevalent. Today these freshwater relatives of lobster are mainly imported from China, Scandinavia, Poland and Turkey. They taste best from May through August, and may be sold only live or canned. In the case of cooked crayfish, if the tail is rolled inwards, that signals that the crayfish was fresh when cooked. The edible portions are the meat from the tail and claw.

Fritto misto
Fried Seafood

300 g/11 oz fresh anchovies
400 g/14 oz seppioline (small squid),
ready to cook
300 g/11 oz small raw prawns
150 g/5 oz flour
½ tsp salt
2 tbsp olive oil
2 egg whites
freshly ground white pepper
oil for frying
lemon wedges to garnish

Wash the anchovies, squid and prawns and drain well. Cut the squid in half. Mix the flour, salt, olive oil, 200 ml/7 fl oz lukewarm water and some pepper into a smooth dough. Beat the egg whites until they are semi-firm and fold them into the dough. Leave it to rest for 10 minutes.

Heat frying oil to 180°C/355°F. Dip the anchovies, squid and prawns into the batter, one at a time, and fry in portions until golden brown. Drain briefly on paper towels and serve with lemon wedges.

Sorrento Lemons

In the seventeenth century, Jesuits on the Sorrento Peninsula and in the Massa Lubrense municipality on the Amalfi Coast began to cultivate a lemon with especially superb qualities, the *limone di massa* or Sorrento lemon, which differs from other lemons in both shape and flavour.

These shiny, bright yellow, oval lemons are characterized by very juicy fruit that has considerable acidity as well as a touch of sweetness.

Sorrento lemons now carry the IGP stamp of quality (Protected Geographical Indication). Their pleasant tartness harmoniously rounds out the flavour of fish and seafood.

Involtini in umido

Involtini in umido
Veal Roulades with Ham

8 thin veal cutlets, 100 g/3½ oz each
50 g/1¾ oz grated pecorino cheese
8 thin slices prosciutto di San Daniele
2 tbsp butter
2 tbsp olive oil
1 onion, finely chopped
1 garlic clove, finely chopped
1 tbsp tomato purée
125 ml/4 fl oz Marsala
125 ml/4 fl oz veal stock
2 tomatoes, diced
1 small sprig sage
flour for coating
salt and pepper

Pound the cutlets thin between two layers of clingfilm and place them side by side on a work surface. Season with salt and pepper. Sprinkle the pecorino over them and top each with a slice of prosciutto. Roll up the cutlets and secure with cocktail sticks, then salt and pepper the roulades and coat with flour.

Heat the butter and oil in a pan and brown the roulades on all sides. Remove from the pan and set aside. Sauté the onion, garlic and tomato purée in the same pan. Deglaze with the wine, stirring to loosen the pan drippings, and pour in the stock. Add the veal roulades, tomatoes and sage to the pan and bring to the boil. Cover and cook on low heat for 20 minutes. Then remove the veal from the pan and keep hot on a serving platter. Remove the sage from the sauce, bring it to the boil, and season with salt and pepper. Pour the sauce over the veal roulades.

Costolette alla milanese
Milanese Veal Chops

4 veal chops, 200 g/7 oz each
2 eggs
100 g/3½ oz breadcrumbs
60 g/2 oz clarified butter
flour for coating
salt and pepper
1 lemon, cut into wedges

Wash the chops, pat them dry, and rub with salt and pepper. Whisk the eggs. Coat the chops first in flour, then in whisked egg and finally in breadcrumbs. Press the breading firmly in place.

Heat the clarified butter in a large frying pan, add the chops and fry on medium heat for 5 to 6 minutes per side until golden brown. Serve the lemon wedges with the veal chops.

Ossobuco alla milanese
Milanese-style
Ossobuco

*4 slices veal shank,
each ca. 4 cm/1½ inches thick*

50 g/1¾ oz butter

125 ml/4 fl oz white wine

400 g/14 oz canned tomato purée

1 garlic clove

1 tbsp grated lemon peel

2 tbsp finely chopped parsley

flour for coating

salt

freshly ground pepper

Wash the meat slices and pat dry with paper towels. Then rub with salt and pepper and coat with flour, shaking off any excess.

Melt the butter in a deep frying pan and brown the veal slices on both sides. Deglaze the pan with the wine, then reduce slightly. Stir in the tomato purée and season with salt and pepper. Cover the pan and stew the meat on low heat for at least 1½ hours, turning the slices over several times in the tomato sauce as they cook. When the meat begins to separate from the bone, it Is done. Finely chop the garlic and combine it with the lemon peel and parsley. Sprinkle over the sliced meat just before serving.

Beef

Tournedos alla Rossini are still famous today and unite three extravagant products on a single plate: fillet of beef, foie gras and truffles. There are two versions of the story explaining the genesis of the recipe. According to the first, the chef at La Maison Dorée Restaurant invented the dish and dedicated it to Rossini. The second version goes like this: when Rossini's chef wanted to try out the new recipe, the maestro required him to prepare it in the dining room so that he and his guests could watch. But the chef explained that it would embarrass him to cook in front of all those people, to which Rossini responded, 'Very well then – just turn your back to me'.

Tournedos alla Rossini
Tournedos à la Rossini

4 thick beef fillet steaks
2 tbsp olive oil
2 tbsp butter
4 slices white bread, toasted
4 slices pâté de foie gras
4 tbsp Madeira
1 small truffle
salt
freshly ground pepper

Tie the fillet steaks into rounds with kitchen twine. Heat the oil and butter and brown the meat on medium heat for about 3 minutes per side. Season with salt and pepper. Cut each slice of toast into the shape of a tournedo, place the meat on it and set on a heated platter. Top with pâté de foie gras. Deglaze the pan with the Madeira and pour over the meat. Finely grate the truffle over the tournedos.

Brasato alla milanese
Milanese-style Roast Beef

Serves six

1 kg/2 lb 4 oz beef roast
2 garlic cloves
1 carrot
2 celery sticks
1 kohlrabi
2 onions
2 tbsp olive oil
2 tbsp butter
1 bay leaf
1 small sprig thyme
1 clove
300 ml/11 fl oz Barolo or other strong red wine
500 g/1 lb 2 oz tomatoes
300 ml/11 fl oz meat stock
3 tbsp finely chopped parsley
salt
freshly ground pepper

Wash the meat and pat it dry. Peel and slice the garlic. Cut into the meat with a sharp knife and insert the garlic slices into the openings. Season the meat with salt and pepper. Wash or peel and finely dice the carrot, celery, kohlrabi and onions.

Heat the olive oil and butter in an iron casserole and brown the meat on all sides on medium heat.

Add the bay leaf, thyme and clove to the casserole. Deglaze with the red wine and reduce slightly.

Peel and quarter the tomatoes, remove the seeds and roughly chop the flesh. Add the tomatoes to the meat, pour in some of the stock and bring to the boil. Cover the casserole and stew for at least 2 hours over low heat. Baste the meat from time to time with the stewing liquid, and gradually add the remaining stock.

When the roast has finished cooking, remove it from the casserole. Pour the stewing liquid through a fine sieve into a small saucepan, bring to the boil again, and season the sauce to taste with salt and pepper. Slice the roast and place it on a heated serving platter. Pour the hot sauce over it and sprinkle with the chopped parsley.

Barding

Beef rump steak, bacon and aromatic herbs are needed for a brasato.

Wash the meat, pat it dry and rub it with salt, pepper and chopped herbs.

Then cover the meat on all sides with thin slices of pork fat or bacon.

To secure the pork fat, tie up the meat lengthways with kitchen twine.

Then wrap the kitchen twine around your hand, loop it around the meat and pull tight.

Repeat this step until the meat is fully wrapped. Fasten the twine with a knot.

Slowly stew the roast in stock or wine. Leave it to rest a few minutes before carving.

Remove the twine and cut the meat into uniform slices with a sharp carving knife.

Involtini alla barese
Beef Roulades with Pecorino

8 thin slices of beef, 100 g/3½ oz each
80 g/3 oz chopped stoned green olives
8 slices coppa ham
80 g/3 oz medium-aged
pecorino cheese, shaved
2 tbsp olive oil
1 onion, finely chopped
1 garlic clove, finely chopped
1 tbsp tomato purée
100 ml/3½ fl oz dry red wine
250 ml/9 fl oz beef stock
salt
freshly ground pepper
1 sprig sage

Wash the sliced beef, pat it dry and poun
flat. Finely dice the olives. Lightly season th
meat with salt and pepper on both sides an
cover each slice with a slice of ham. Sprinkl
olives and pecorino on the ham. Roll up th
roulades and tie them with kitchen twine.

Heat the olive oil in a large frying pan an
brown the roulades on medium heat. Add th
onion, garlic and tomato purée. Then deglaz
the pan with the wine, stirring to loosen th
pan drippings, and reduce the liquid.

Pour in the stock, add the sage sprig, plac
the lid so that it half covers the pan an
braise for 30 to 40 minutes on low heat. The
take the roulades out of the pan, remove th
twine, and keep the meat warm. Bring th
sauce to the boil and season to taste wit
salt and pepper. Serve the roulades on heate
plates with sauce poured over them.

Filetto all'alloro
Fillet of Beef in Laurel Wreath

4 beef fillet steaks, 250 g/9 oz each
4 tsp spicy mustard
12 fresh bay leaves
3 tbsp olive oil
1 tbsp peppercorns, coarsely crushed
60 ml/2 fl oz Italian brandy
salt

Preheat the oven to 130°C/265°F/gas mark ½. Brush the edges of the steaks with the mustard. Place 3 bay leaves around each steak and secure with kitchen twine. Season with salt.

Heat the olive oil in an ovenproof pan and thoroughly brown the steaks on both sides, then cook in the oven for 15 to 20 minutes.

Place the steaks on heated plates. Pour off the frying fat and sprinkle the peppercorns in the pan. Pour in the brandy, heat slightly, then flambé. Drizzle the brandy sauce over the fillets and serve immediately.

Favourite Lamb Dishes

Agnello all'uovo e limone
Lamb Goulash with Egg and Lemon

800 g/1 lb 12 oz lamb shoulder
2 tbsp flour
1 onion
60 g/2 oz pork fat
2 tbsp oil
300 ml/11 fl oz white wine
125 ml/4 fl oz stock
juice of 1 lemon
2 egg yolks
1 garlic clove
salt
freshly ground pepper
grated lemon peel for seasoning

Rinse the lamb, pat it dry and cut into 3-cm/1-inch cubes. Salt and pepper the lamb, then sprinkle with the flour. Peel the onion. Finely dice it and the pork fat.

Heat the oil in an iron casserole and fry the pork fat. Add the lamb in portions and brown it, stirring frequently. Add the onion and fry until translucent. Deglaze with half of the wine, scraping the pan to loosen the drippings. Once the wine has reduced, add the stock, cover the casserole and simmer for about 1 hour on low heat. Gradually add the rest of the wine.

Remove the pieces of cooked lamb with a slotted spoon and keep warm on a serving plate. Whisk together the lemon juice and egg yolk. Put the garlic through a press and add it to the egg yolk mixture. Bring the pan juices to the boil again and add the egg-lemon mixture, stirring continuously, but do not allow the sauce to boil. Season it to taste with salt, pepper and lemon peel. Pour over the lamb and serve hot.

Filetto alle verdure
Fillet of Lamb on Vegetable Pasta

2 carrots
2 small courgettes
100 g/3½ oz mushrooms
4 lamb fillets, 130 g/4½ oz each
2 tbsp clarified butter
400 ml/14 fl oz lamb stock
200 ml/7 fl oz double cream
250 g/9 oz tagliatelle
4 tbsp butter
salt
freshly ground pepper

Peel the carrots and slice into long strips with a vegetable peeler. Wash the courgettes and cut them lengthways into thin strips. Bring a saucepan of lightly salted water to the boil and blanch the vegetable strips for 2 minutes. Refresh them in cold water, then drain.

Preheat the oven to 100°C/210°F/gas mark 6. Clean and finely slice the mushrooms. Rinse the lamb fillets and pat dry. Salt and pepper the meat. Heat the clarified butter in a frying pan and brown the fillets on both sides. Place on an ovenproof plate and roast for 20 minutes.

Pour the fat from the pan. Pour in the lamb stock and stir to dissolve the pan drippings in the stock. Add the cream and simmer until the sauce is reduced by half. Bring a large saucepan of salted water to the boil and cook the tagliatelle until al dente.

Melt the butter in a second pan and gently sauté the mushrooms. Add the vegetable strips to heat them up. Drain the pasta, then combine it with the vegetable strips and mushrooms. Season with salt and pepper.

Remove the meat from the oven and slice it diagonally. Stir the meat juice into the sauce and heat it up. Serve the pasta on heated plates topped with the meat, with a liberal serving of sauce over it.

Spezzatino di castrato
Mutton Ragout

1 kg/2 lb 4 oz mutton, shoulder cut
100 ml/3½ fl oz white wine vinegar
2 sprigs rosemary
2–3 garlic cloves
5 tbsp olive oil
400 g/14 oz canned peeled tomatoes
2 bay leaves
200 ml/7 fl oz white wine
salt
freshly ground pepper
sugar

Rinse the mutton, pat dry, then remove any skin, tendons and fat. Cut the meat into bite-sized chunks. In a large saucepan, bring to the boil 1 litre/1¾ pints of water, the vinegar and 1 rosemary sprig. Add the meat cubes to the pot and cook for about 10 minutes, then remove them and drain well.

Chop the garlic and the leaves from the second rosemary sprig. Heat the olive oil in an iron casserole, add the meat cubes and brown on all sides. Add the garlic and rosemary and sauté briefly. Season liberally with salt and pepper. Drain the tomatoes and add them to the meat with the bay leaves. Pour on the white wine, then bring everything to the boil. Cover the ragout and stew on low heat for around 1½ hours, stirring occasionally. Remove the lid 15 minutes before the end of cooking time so the sauce can thicken. Adjust the seasoning with salt, pepper and sugar before serving.

Agnello con olive
Lamb with Black Olives

800 g/1 lb 12 oz lamb
2 sprigs rosemary
1 bay leaf
½ tsp black peppercorns
2 garlic cloves
100 ml/3½ fl oz olive oil
200 g/7 oz chickpeas
1 onion
1 leek
2 carrots
150 g/5 oz black olives
2 tomatoes
flour for coating
1 litre/1¾ pints vegetable stock
1 tsp grated orange rind
freshly ground pepper
1 tbsp finely chopped sage

Cut the meat into bite-sized chunks and place it in a bowl. Add the rosemary leaves, bay leaf, peppercorns and garlic, then pour on the olive oil. Cover with clingfilm and marinate in the refrigerator overnight. Turn the meat several times in the seasoned oil. Soak the chickpeas overnight in plenty of water.

The next day, chop the onion, leek and carrots into small pieces. Set aside a few olives for garnish; stone and roughly chop the rest. Peel and quarter the tomatoes, remove the seeds, and cut into fine dice.

Remove the meat from the herbed oil and drain. Coat it with a little flour, shaking off any excess. Strain the herbed oil through a sieve into a bowl. Pour the water off the chickpeas and also drain thoroughly.

Heat 3 tablespoons of the herbed oil in an iron casserole and lightly brown the meat in it. Add the onion and tomato and cook for a few minutes, then stir in the chickpeas. Pour in the stock and bring to the boil. Cover the casserole and simmer for 30 minutes over low heat, then add the olives, leeks, carrots and orange peel. Stew for another 30 minutes.

Season the lamb ragout with salt and pepper. Serve on heated plates, sprinkled with sage and garnished with whole olives.

Favourite Pork Dishes

Spezzatino di maiale
Pork Goulash

600 g/1 lb 5 oz lean pork
2–3 tbsp olive oil
1 tsp fennel seeds
5 garlic cloves, finely chopped
1 fresh red chilli, finely chopped
300 g/11 oz tomatoes, peeled and diced
salt
freshly ground pepper

Wash the meat, pat it dry and cut into bit sized pieces. Heat the olive oil in an iron cass role, then add the fennel seeds and garlic it. Season the meat with salt and pepper.

Brown the meat on all sides in the h olive oil. As soon as the meat browns, add t chilli and tomatoes. Cover the pot and ste over low heat for about 1 hour, adding a litt warm water as needed.

Polpette dei preti
Priests' Meatloaf

1 pork caul
100 g/3½ oz prosciutto
100 g/3½ oz mortadella
soup vegetables such as carrots, celery
or other root vegetables
1 onion
400 g/14 oz mixed minced meat
1 egg
3 tbsp breadcrumbs
75 g/2½ oz grated Parmesan
1 tbsp clarified butter
1 litre/1¾ pints hot milk
1 garlic clove
1 bay leaf
salt
freshly ground pepper

Rinse the pork caul for 30 minutes, then drain. Finely dice the prosciutto and mortadella. Wash and roughly chop the soup vegetables. Peel and finely dice the onion.

Combine the minced meat with the prosciutto, mortadella, egg, breadcrumbs and Parmesan. Season with salt and pepper. Form the meat into a loaf. Spread out the drained pork caul, place the meatloaf on it and wrap with the caul.

Heat the clarified butter in an iron casserole and briefly brown the meatloaf on all sides. Remove it from the pot, then lightly brown the soup vegetables and onion in the pan drippings. Return the meatloaf to the pot and pour on 250 ml/9 fl oz of the hot milk. Mash the garlic clove with a knife and add it to the milk along with the bay leaf. Bring to a boil and simmer, covered, on low heat for about 1 hour. Gradually add the remaining hot milk during that time.

Place the finished meatloaf on a heated platter. Season the sauce with salt and pepper. Serve the meatloaf with the sauce on the side.

Favourite Chicken and Turkey Dishes

Pollo alla salvia
Sage Chicken

4 boneless chicken breasts with skin
2 slices prosciutto
8 sage leaves
1 garlic clove
1 tbsp fennel seeds, ground in a mortar
4 tbsp olive oil
½ lime, sliced
salt
freshly ground pepper

Preheat the oven to 170°C/340°F/gas mark 3. Gently loosen the skin on each chicken breast and place half a slice of prosciutto and 1 sage leaf underneath it. Cut the remaining sage leaves into strips. Peel and finely chop the garlic. Season the meat with salt and pepper, then rub the fennel seeds and garlic into it.

Heat the olive oil in a frying pan. Fry the meat on the skin side first, then on the other side. Remove from the pan and lay in a baking dish. Pour the pan drippings over the chicken, then place the lime slices and remaining sage leaves on top. Cook in the oven for about 30 minutes, then serve on a heated platter.

Pollo alla Marengo
Marengo Chicken

1 chicken, ready to cook
3 tbsp olive oil
125 ml/4 fl oz white wine
50 g/1¾ oz pearl onions
2 garlic cloves
2 tbsp flour
500 ml/18 fl oz poultry stock
4 small vine tomatoes
200 g/7 oz small mushrooms
4 crayfish tails, cooked
1 tbsp finely chopped parsley
salt
freshly ground pepper

Wash the chicken, pat it dry and cut it into 4 portions. Rub generous amounts of salt and pepper into the skin. Heat the olive oil in an iron casserole and brown the chicken quarters on all sides. Deglaze with the wine, then cover the pot and simmer for 10 minutes.

Peel the pearl onions and garlic. Cut the pearl onions in half and finely chop the garlic. Add both to the chicken, dust with the flour and cook briefly. Then pour in the poultry stock. Cover the pot and simmer for 20 minutes on medium heat.

Meanwhile, peel the tomatoes and cut into quarters. Cut the mushrooms in half. Add the vegetables to the chicken and season with salt and pepper. If necessary, add a little more wine. Simmer on low heat for another 25 to 30 minutes.

Add the crayfish tails and warm them in the sauce. Sprinkle the parsley over the chicken and serve on heated plates.

Pollo alla diavola
Spicy Chicken

2 dried red chillies, chopped
2 tbsp lemon juice
3 tbsp orange juice
500 ml/18 fl oz white wine
1 bay leaf
1 chicken, ready to cook
salt
freshly ground pepper

In a bowl, stir the chillies, citrus juices and wine together, then crumble the bay leaf into the mixture.

Cut the neck and wing tips off the chicken. Cut through the chicken along the breastbone and pull it open. Then carefully pound it as flat as possible without damaging the bones in the process. Lay the chicken in a bowl and pour the wine marinade over it. Cover and marinate in the refrigerator for a day, turning it over once.

Remove the chicken from the marinade, pat it dry and rub salt and pepper into it. Set under the grill or barbecue over charcoal for about 40 minutes until crisp and brown, turning periodically.

The Battle of Marengo

Marengo, a little village in the Italian province of Alessandria, set the stage for the historic battle of 14 June 1800, in which Napoleon scored a decisive victory over the Austrians. When the glorious commander then clamoured for something to eat, Dunant, his chef and a native of Switzerland, had to improvise, because he had lost all of his provisions and baggage in the heat of battle. So he sent soldiers off in search of food.

They returned, bringing him chicken, tomatoes, mushrooms and crayfish that Dunant ingeniously combined into a very delicious dish, Polla alla Marengo. This fortuitous meal is said to have met with the French emperor's enthusiastic approval, and it has not lost any of its freshness or spontaneity in the past two centuries. Today gourmets in France, Italy and elsewhere love this uncommon recipe (left).

Pollo alla cacciatora
Chicken Cacciatore

1 chicken, ready to cook
2 tbsp olive oil
50 g/1¾ oz pancetta, diced
1 white onion, finely chopped
125 ml/4 fl oz white wine
4 tomatoes
250 ml/9 fl oz meat stock
salt
freshly ground pepper

Wash the chicken, pat it dry and cut it into 8 pieces. Rub generous amounts of salt and pepper into the skin. Heat the olive oil in an iron casserole and fry the pancetta and onion until the onions are translucent. Add the chicken pieces and brown on all sides. Deglaze the pan with the white wine and simmer for 5 minutes.

Peel and quarter the tomatoes, remove the seeds, and cut into small dice. Add to the chicken, then pour in the meat stock. Cover the pot and stew for 30 to 40 minutes. Season to taste with salt and pepper before serving.

Pollo alla griglia
Barbecued Chicken

1 maize-fed chicken,
ca. 1.2 kg/2 lb 10 oz, ready to cook
2 tsp grated lemon rind
3 garlic cloves, finely sliced
juice of 3 lemons
6 tbsp olive oil
salt
coarsely ground pepper

Wash the chicken, pat it dry and cut it in half lengthways. Lay the chicken halves in a bowl and season them with pepper. Spread the lemon rind and garlic over the chicken. Pour on the lemon juice and olive oil, then cover and marinate overnight in the refrigerator.

The next day, take the chicken halves out of the marinade and drain. Season the meat with salt and barbecue slowly over charcoal or set under a medium grill until crisp on both sides. Brush the chicken occasionally with the marinade while grilling.

Pollo al vino bianco
Chicken in White Wine

1 chicken, ca. 1.3 kg/3 lb,
ready to cook
2 tbsp olive oil
150 g/5 oz pancetta, diced
5 shallots, diced
1 tbsp flour
750 ml/1⅓ pints white wine
1 sprig rosemary
salt
freshly ground pepper

Wash the chicken, pat it dry and cut it into portions. Rub each piece with salt and pepper. Preheat the oven to 175°C/350°F/gas mark 4.

Heat the olive oil in a roasting tin and brown the meat on all sides. Add the pancetta and shallots and fry. Dust with the flour and pour in the wine. Add the rosemary sprig. Cover the roasting tin and put it in the oven for 30 minutes.

After that time, remove the lid from the roasting tin and return the chicken to the oven to continue cooking until the wine has nearly evaporated. Remove the rosemary sprig before serving.

Tacchino ripieno
Turkey with Stuffing

Serves six

1 young turkey, ca. 3.5 kg/7–8 lb,
ready to cook
100 g/3½ oz pancetta, diced
2 onions, finely chopped
2 tsp dried thyme
2 celery sticks, diced
3 apples, diced
50 g/1¾ oz sultanas
50 g/1¾ oz currants
100 g/3½ oz dried fruits
(apricots, cherries, prunes), diced
2 eggs
75 g/2½ oz breadcrumbs
2 tbsp olive oil, plus extra for greasing
500 ml/18 fl oz poultry stock
125 ml/4 fl oz red wine
salt
freshly ground pepper

Wash the turkey and pat dry. Generously rub it with salt and pepper, inside and out. Preheat the oven to 175°C/350°F/gas mark 4 and grease a roasting tin with olive oil.

Render the pancetta in a frying pan. Add the onions and sauté until translucent. Stir in the thyme and celery and sauté a few minutes. Remove the pan from the stove. Combine the onion mixture with the apples, sultanas, currants and dried fruits. Cool slightly, then stir in the eggs and breadcrumbs. Season the stuffing with salt and pepper.

Fill the turkey with the stuffing and close the cavity with wooden skewers. Place the turkey in the roasting tin. Brush the turkey with olive oil. Roast for 3½ to 4 hours, basting from time to time with the poultry stock.

When the turkey is done, remove it from the roasting tin and keep it warm. Pour the cooking juices into a saucepan and skim off the fat. Add the red wine, then boil for several minutes. Season the sauce with salt and pepper and serve with the turkey.

Favourite Vegetable Dishes

Broccoli strascinati
Broccoli with Anchovy Sauce

1 kg/2 lb 4 oz broccoli

4 anchovy fillets in oil

100 ml/3½ fl oz olive oil

salt

freshly ground pepper

Clean the broccoli and separate it into small florets. Peel the stalks, halve or quarter them according to their thickness and slice finely.

Bring a saucepan of salted water to the boil and cook the stalks for about 10 minutes, then add the florets and simmer for another 8 to 10 minutes.

Rinse the anchovies in cold, flowing water, then pat them dry and chop finely.

Heat the olive oil in a deep frying pan. Add the anchovies and mash them into a paste. Drain the broccoli well, then combine with the anchovy sauce. Season with pepper and serve hot.

Carote al Marsala
Carrots with Marsala

500 g/1 lb 2 oz carrots
1 white onion
2 tbsp olive oil
1 tsp soft brown sugar
4 tbsp Marsala
2 tbsp pine kernels
salt
freshly ground pepper

Peel and slice the carrots. Peel the onion and dice it. Heat the olive oil in a saucepan and fry the onion. Add the carrots and cook lightly, then sprinkle with the sugar, turn the heat on high and caramelize the vegetables. Add 100 ml/3½ fl oz water and season with salt and pepper. Over low heat, cook the carrots for an additional 10 minutes until the water has evaporated. Pour the Marsala over the vegetables and reduce once again.

Heat a frying pan and dry-roast the pine kernels until golden brown. Before serving, sprinkle them over the carrots.

Cavolo in umido
Stewed Savoy Cabbage

1 small Savoy cabbage
2 tbsp olive oil
1 tbsp butter
1 small onion, finely chopped
juice of 1 lemon
250 ml/9 fl oz vegetable stock
2 bay leaves
⅛ tsp ground allspice
salt
freshly ground pepper
freshly grated nutmeg

Clean the cabbage, cut it in quarters and remove the stalk with a wedge-shaped cut so that the leaves remain attached.

Heat the olive oil and butter in a large saucepan and sauté the onion. Add the cabbage quarters and briefly fry. Sprinkle with the lemon juice and pour the stock over the cabbage. Add the bay leaves and season with the allspice, salt, pepper and nutmeg. Cover the pot and braise the cabbage on medium heat for 25 to 30 minutes.

For the sauce, first peel the tomatoes, remove the seeds and chop the flesh into cubes.

Sauté the onion, garlic and tomatoes in olive oil, then add the wine.

Briefly blanch the Savoy cabbage leaves in lightly salted water.

Remove the thick rib in the centre with a wedge-shaped cut.

Place a portion of the rice-mozzarella filling on the centre of each leaf.

Then fold the top part of the leaf over the filling.

Next, fold the sides of the cabbage leaf over the filling and roll it up.

Fry the roulades in olive oil and lay them in the tomato sauce.

Involtini di cavolo verza
Stuffed Cabbage

750 g/1 lb 10 oz plum tomatoes
60 ml/2 fl oz olive oil
1 white onion, finely chopped
2 garlic cloves, finely chopped
125 ml/4 fl oz white wine
1 pinch sugar
8 large Savoy cabbage leaves
200 g/7 oz buffalo mozzarella
200 g/7 oz cooked rice
1 egg
2 tbsp finely chopped parsley
salt
freshly ground pepper

Peel and quarter the tomatoes, remove the seeds, and cut into dice. Heat 3 tablespoons of the olive oil in a saucepan and sauté the onion and garlic. Add the tomatoes and wine, then season with the sugar and salt and pepper. Simmer on low heat for 20 minutes.

Bring a large saucepan of salted water to the boil and briefly blanch the cabbage leaves. Remove them with a slotted spoon, refresh in cold water and place in a strainer to drain. For the filling, finely dice the mozzarella and mix it with the rice, egg and parsley. Season to taste with salt and pepper.

Place the cabbage leaves on a work surface and place a spoonful of filling in the middle of each leaf. Fold over the edges, starting at the top, and roll into a bundle. If necessary, tie with kitchen string.

Heat the remaining olive oil in a pan and briefly fry the roulades on both sides. Lay the roulades in the tomato sauce with the seams facing down. Cover the pan and stew about 40 minutes on low heat. If the sauce becomes too thick, add a little water or wine as needed.

Favourite Vegetable Dishes from the Oven

Finocchi gratinati
Fennel Gratin

4 fennel bulbs
1 tbsp lemon juice
2 tbsp butter, plus extra for greasing
2 tbsp flour
500 ml/18 fl oz warm milk
100 ml/3½ fl oz double cream
2 tbsp white wine
125 g/4½ oz grated fontina cheese
50 g/1¾ oz pine kernels
salt
freshly ground pepper
freshly grated nutmeg

Remove the fennel greens and set aside. Slice the bulbs about 5 mm/¼ inch thick and blanch in boiling salted water, with the lemon juice, for 3 minutes. Remove the fennel with a slotted spoon and refresh in cold water, then drain. Preheat the oven to 175°C/350°F/gas mark 4 and grease a baking dish with butter.

In a heavy saucepan, melt the butter, stir in the flour and cook briefly. While stirring continuously, add the warm milk and cream and leave the sauce to thicken. Blend in the white wine and season to taste with salt, pepper and nutmeg.

Lay the fennel slices in the baking dish. Pour the sauce over the fennel and sprinkle the cheese on top. Bake for about 25 minutes or until golden brown. Heat a frying pan and dry-roast the pine kernels until golden brown. Finely chop the fennel greens. Before serving, sprinkle the greens and roasted pine kernels over the gratin.

Peperoni ripieni
Stuffed Peppers

2 red peppers
2 yellow peppers
7 anchovy fillets in oil
4 tomatoes
75 ml/2½ fl oz olive oil,
plus extra for greasing
1 white onion, finely chopped
2 tbsp finely chopped parsley
2 tbsp grated Parmesan
2 tbsp breadcrumbs
salt
freshly ground pepper

Wash the peppers, halve them lengthways, and remove the cores. Rinse the anchovies under cold water, pat dry, then chop them finely. Peel and quarter the tomatoes, remove the seeds, and cut into dice. Preheat the oven to 230°C/450°F/gas mark 8 and grease a baking dish with olive oil.

Heat 2 tablespoons of the olive oil and fry the anchovies and onion. Tip them into a bowl and mix with the tomatoes, parsley, Parmesan and breadcrumbs. Season the mixture with salt and pepper, then fill the pepper halves with it.

Place the stuffed peppers side by side in the baking dish. Cover it with aluminium foil and bake for 15 minutes. Remove the foil, sprinkle the peppers with the remaining olive oil and bake for another 10 to 15 minutes. Serve hot or cold.

Cavolini di Bruxelles alla panna
Scalloped Brussels Sprouts

1 kg/2 lb 4 oz Brussels sprouts
4 tbsp butter, plus extra for greasing
1 onion, finely chopped
1 garlic clove, finely chopped
250 ml/9 fl oz vegetable stock
2 eggs
250 ml/9 fl oz double cream
60 g/2 oz grated Parmesan
salt
freshly ground pepper
freshly grated nutmeg

Preheat the oven to 175°C/350°F/gas mark 4 and grease a baking dish with butter. Trim the Brussels sprouts. Melt half the butter in a saucepan and sauté the onions and garlic until the onions are translucent. Add the Brussels sprouts, season with salt, pepper and nutmeg, and pour on the stock. Cover the pan and simmer on medium heat for 15 minutes.

Pour the Brussels sprouts and cooking liquid into the baking dish. Whisk the eggs and cream together and pour over the Brussels sprouts. Sprinkle with the Parmesan and dot with the remaining butter. Bake for about 20 minutes.

Wash the beetroots, pat dry and wrap individually in aluminium foil.

After baking, unwrap the beetroots and leave them to cool slightly.

Barbabietole al forno
Baked Red Beetroots
with Balsamic Vinaigrette

500 g/1 lb 2 oz red beetroots
2 tbsp balsamic vinegar
1 tsp mustard
5 tbsp olive oil
salt and pepper
1 small handful fresh mint

Preheat the oven to 200°C/390°F/gas mark 6. Wash and dry the beetroots and wrap each one individually in aluminium foil. Place them on a baking tray and bake 40 to 60 minutes, depending on their size.

When done, remove the beetroots from the foil, cool, then peel. Beetroots stain skin dramatically, so kitchen gloves are recommended. Slice the beetroots and arrange them on a serving platter.

Whisk the vinegar, mustard and olive oil together, season with salt and pepper, and pour over the beetroots. Wash the mint, pat dry and pluck the leaves. Cut them into narrow strips and sprinkle over the beetroots.

Potatoes

In Italy, potatoes are not merely a filling side dish, but – like all other vegetables – are significant in their own right. The nutritious tubers are fried with aromatic herbs, or used as the main ingredient in casseroles and vegetable timbales. Especially in northern Italy, potatoes also make their way to the table in the form of gnocchi.

Spanish conquistadors 'discovered' the potato in the Andes in the sixteenth century. The Incas prepared dishes out of these tubers that greatly appealed to the Spaniards. Since at first sight the invaders thought that these new vegetables growing underground were truffles, they called the unknown food Incan *taratoufli*.

Timballo verde
Vegetable Timbale

600 g/1 lb 5 oz baking potatoes
500 g/1 lb 2 oz leaf spinach
1 tbsp olive oil
1 white onion, finely chopped
2 bunches parsley
4 eggs
100 ml/3½ fl oz double cream
100 g/3½ oz grated Parmesan
3 tbsp butter, plus extra for greasing
salt
freshly ground pepper
freshly grated nutmeg

Bring a large saucepan of salted water to the boil. Wash the potatoes and cook them, in their skins, for about 20 minutes.

Thoroughly wash the spinach, removing any wilted leaves and coarse stalks. Heat the olive oil in a frying pan and briefly sauté the onion, then add the dripping-wet spinach. Cover the pan and steam for 2 to 3 minutes. Pour off the water and drain the spinach. Peel and mash the potatoes while still hot.

Preheat the oven to 175°C/350°F/gas mark 4 and grease a round baking dish with butter. Wash the parsley, pat it dry and pluck the leaves. Purée the parsley and spinach with a hand-held mixer. Season with salt, pepper and nutmeg.

Whisk the eggs and cream together and stir into the mashed potatoes. Stir in the spinach purée and half of the Parmesan, and season again with salt and pepper.

Fill the baking dish with the potato-spinach mixture. Sprinkle the remaining Parmesan and dot the butter on top. Bake for about 25 minutes or until golden brown.

Peel the cooked potatoes and mash them while they are still hot.

Thoroughly wash the spinach, removing any wilted leaves or coarse stalks.

Purée the parsley and spinach with a hand-held mixer until smooth.

Stir the spinach purée, eggs and cream into the mashed potatoes.

Fill a round baking dish with the potato-spinach mixture and bake.

Patate al rosmarino
Rosemary Potatoes

750 g/1 lb 10 oz potatoes
3 garlic cloves
3 sprigs rosemary
75 ml/2½ fl oz olive oil,
plus extra for greasing
salt
freshly ground pepper

Wash and peel the potatoes and cut them into small cubes. Peel and roughly chop the garlic. Pluck the leaves from the rosemary and roughly chop them as well. Preheat the oven to 200°C/390°F/gas mark 6. Grease a flat baking dish with olive oil.

Place a layer of potatoes on the base of the baking dish. Season with some of the garlic and rosemary, salt and pepper. Repeat this procedure until all the ingredients have been used. Drizzle the olive oil over the top and bake for about 45 minutes, tossing the potatoes several times. Serve in the baking dish while hot.

Favourite
Egg Dishes

Frittata con prezzemolo
Frittata with Parsley

1 bunch flat-leaf parsley
6 eggs
4 tbsp olive oil
salt
freshly ground pepper

Rinse and pat dry the parsley, then roughly chop the leaves. Beat the eggs in a bowl with some salt and pepper until foamy, then blend in the parsley.

Heat the olive oil in a heavy frying pan until it starts to smoke. Pour in the eggs and smooth the surface with a wooden spatula. Reduce the heat to low and leave the eggs to thicken.

As soon as the frittata begins to brown on the underside, use a lid or plate to turn over the omelette carefully. Cook the other side until it is golden brown. Cut the frittata into 4 slices and serve while hot or warm.

The classic frittata is prepared with fresh eggs, parsley, salt and pepper.

Beat the eggs with salt and pepper until they are foamy, and then stir in parsley.

Heat olive oil in a frying pan and pour in the eggs.

Fry the omelette on both sides until golden brown

Frittata di carciofi
Artichoke Frittata

6 artichoke hearts in oil
1 handful rocket
6 eggs
3 tbsp double cream
1 tbsp finely chopped parsley
2 tbsp olive oil
1 tbsp butter
1 onion, finely diced
1 garlic clove, finely diced
salt
freshly ground pepper

Drain and quarter the artichoke hearts. Thoroughly wash the rocket, removing any wilting leaves and coarse stalks, and chop the leaves.

Whisk the eggs and cream together, then season with salt and pepper and stir in the chopped parsley.

Heat the olive oil and butter in a non-stick frying pan. Fry the onion and garlic until the onion is translucent. Add the artichokes and cook briefly. Pour the egg-cream mixture over the artichokes and reduce the heat. As soon as the surface solidifies, use a lid or plate to turn over the frittata gently and cook the other side until golden brown.

Serve the frittata hot, or leave to cool and cut it into bite-sized pieces.

Crespelle Basic Recipe

3 eggs
150 g/5 oz flour
250 ml/9 fl oz milk
1 pinch salt
60 g/2 oz butter

Beat the eggs, then stir in the flour and milk to make a thin batter. Season with a pinch of salt. Leave the batter to rest for 30 minutes.

Melt a little butter in a non-stick frying pan and pour in one small ladle of batter. Swivel the pan to distribute the batter evenly. Fry the *crespelle* on both sides until golden brown, then set aside and keep hot. Repeat this procedure to make 8 *crespelle*.

Crespelle al prosciutto di Parma
Crespelle with Prosciutto

8 crespelle (see basic recipe)
3 tbsp olive oil, plus extra for greasing
1 small onion, finely chopped
1 garlic clove, finely chopped
400 g/14 oz canned chopped tomatoes
1 tbsp chopped basil
100 g/3½ oz prosciutto, finely sliced
50 g/1¾ oz grated Parmesan
salt
freshly ground pepper

Prepare the crespelle according to the basic recipe and cool slightly. Heat 2 tablespoons of the olive oil in a frying pan and sauté the onion and garlic until the onion is translucent, then add the tomatoes. Season with the basil, salt and pepper and simmer for 10 minutes. Preheat the oven to 225°C/435°F/gas mark 7 and grease a baking dish with olive oil.

Lay the prosciutto slices on the crespelle, roll them up and arrange side by side in the baking dish. Cover with the tomato sauce and sprinkle with the Parmesan and remaining olive oil. Bake for about 15 minutes.

Crespelle al forno
Crespelle Gratin

8 crespelle (see basic recipe)
300 g/11 oz assorted wild mushrooms
50 g/1¾ oz butter
1 small onion, finely chopped
100 g/3½ oz cooked ham, cut into strips
2 tbsp chopped parsley
500 ml/18 fl oz béchamel sauce
100 g/3½ oz Gorgonzola, crumbled
salt
freshly ground pepper

Prepare the crespelle according to the basic recipe and cool slightly. Wash the mushrooms and cut into thin slices. Preheat the oven to 225°C/435°F/gas mark 7 and grease a baking dish with 1½ tablespoons of the butter.

Heat the remaining butter in a frying pan and sauté the onion until translucent, then add the ham and mushrooms. Stirring constantly, sauté for about 10 minutes until the liquid has thickened. Stir in the parsley and remove the pan from the stovetop.

Season the mushrooms with salt and pepper and place some on each crespelle. Roll them up and arrange side by side in the baking dish. Pour the béchamel sauce over the crespelle and sprinkle with crumbled Gorgonzola. Bake for about 15 minutes.

Desserts

Favourite Desserts

The palette of Italian desserts is as colourful and multi-faceted as the land itself. One could simplify by distinguishing different categories of *dolci*: fruit desserts, creamy desserts and puddings (which are most often turned out of moulds), and frozen or semi-frozen treats. The scale of the recipes ranges from simple to complicated, from unostentatious to elegant – although complicated methods of preparation are no guarantee of a delicious dessert. As in all other areas of the culinary arts, the optimal quality of the products used is of primary importance. Fruits should have reached their full flavour, that is, they should be ripe but not over-ripe. Mousses should always be given enough time to chill, thereby allowing them to firm in the mould.

Most desserts are portioned and served on plates, decorated with herbs, nuts, cream, icing sugar or cocoa. If more than one dessert is served on a single plate, it is important that the flavours harmonize rather than overshadow one another. Neutral accompaniments include a fruit coulis, lady finger biscuits or ice cream, preferably home-made. Always valid is the dictum that a few select ingredients are often preferable to an abundance of unmanageable flavours.

Pere al vino rosso
Pears in Red Wine

750 ml/1⅓ pints full-bodied red wine
250 g/9 oz sugar
1 cinnamon stick
2 cloves
1 kg/2 lb 4 oz small, firm pears

Preheat the oven to 150°C/300°F/gas mark 2. Combine the wine and sugar in a saucepan, add the cinnamon stick and cloves, and bring to the boil.

Place the unpeeled pears, stems facing upwards, in a deep baking dish. Pour the hot spiced wine over the pears and bake for 1 hour or until soft but not falling apart. Remove the dish from the oven and leave the pears to cool in the wine. Slice and serve hot or cold. Cooking time may vary according to type of pear, so test them often.

Fragole all'aceto balsamico
Strawberries with
Balsamic Vinegar

500 g/1 lb 2 oz strawberries
2 tbsp caster sugar
2–3 tbsp high-quality balsamic vinegar
several mint leaves to decorate

Remove the stems from the strawberries and halve or quarter them, according to size. Sprinkle the sugar, then the vinegar over the berries and mix carefully. Cover with clingfilm and leave to rest for at least 1 hour. Before serving, gently mix again and garnish with mint leaves.

Pesche ripiene
Stuffed Peaches

4 firm yellow peaches
1 tbsp lemon juice
75 g/2½ oz crystallized lemon peel
75 g/2½ oz crumbled amaretti
3 tbsp sugar
1 egg yolk
50 ml/1½ fl oz Marsala
8 blanched almonds
250 ml/9 fl oz white wine
butter for greasing

Preheat the oven to 175°C/350°F/gas mark 4 and grease a baking dish with butter.

Cut the peaches in half and carefully twist the halves apart, removing the stones. Sprinkle with the lemon juice.

Finely chop the crystallized lemon peel. Combine it with the amaretti, sugar, egg yolk and Marsala. Fill the peach halves with the mixture and press one almond into the centre of each. Place the peach halves next to each other in the baking dish and pour on the white wine. Bake for 15 to 20 minutes. Serve hot or cold in the wine sauce.

Almonds

Native to the Middle East, the almond tree grows throughout the Mediterranean basin. In antiquity, its fragrant and slightly sweet seeds were already prized not only as a healthy food, but also for their medicinal properties. Almonds contain many valuable fatty acids, vitamins and minerals. In Italy, they are a popular ingredient for a wide range of confections, cakes and other baked goods.

Sugared almonds are traditionally associated with Italian weddings; newlyweds send little packets containing five sugar-covered almonds as a token of thanks for the gifts they receive. The nuts symbolize health, prosperity, fruitfulness, happiness and long life. Sugared almonds from Sulmona in Abruzzo are especially famous. Approximately 500 tons of their sugared almonds are sent throughout the world every year.

Pesche ripiene

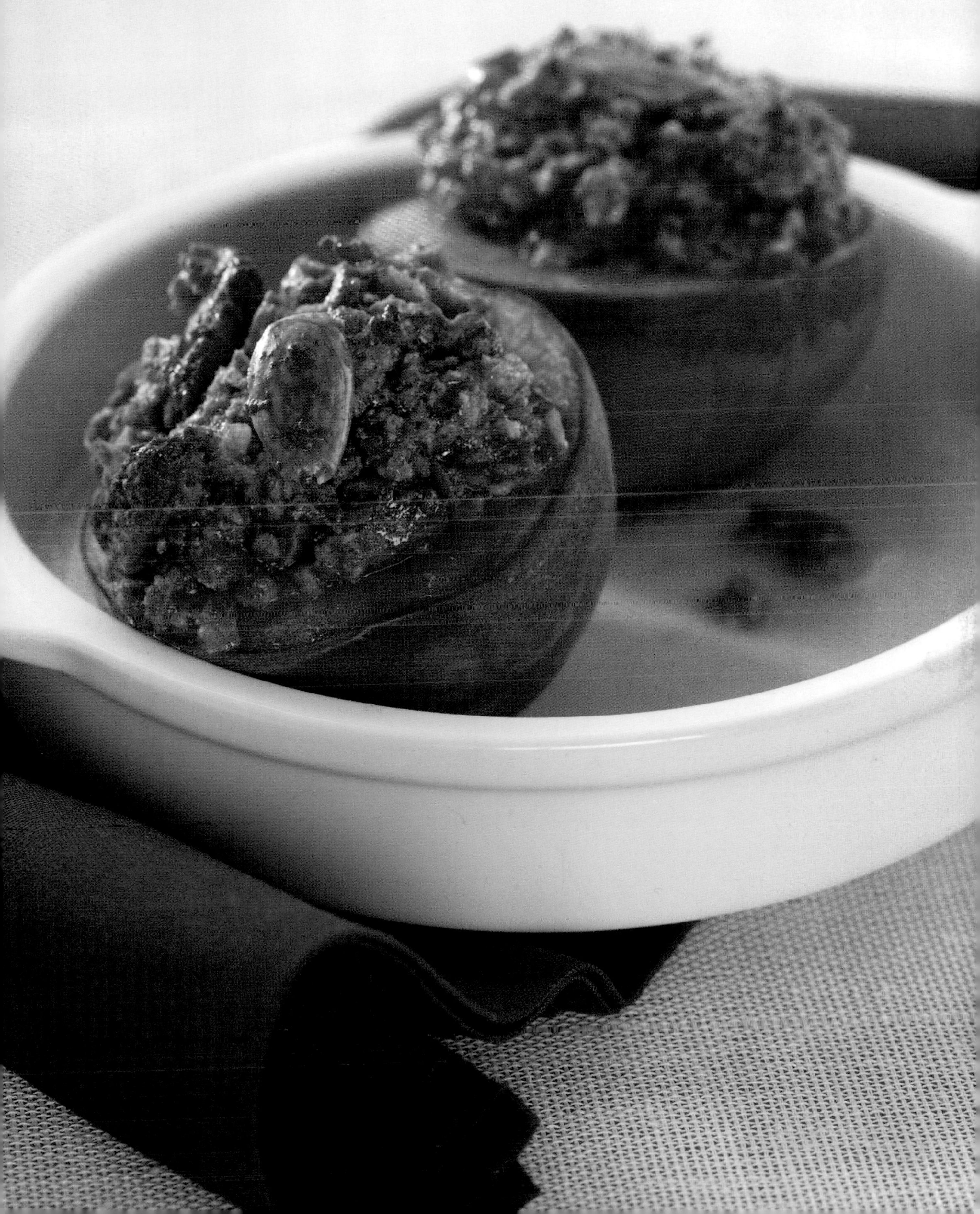

Mele cotte al vino bianco
Apples in White Wine

1 kg/2 lb 4 oz apples
5 tbsp lemon juice
250 ml/ 9 fl oz white wine
200 g/7 oz sugar
1 cinnamon stick
2 cloves

Peel, quarter and core the apples. Cut them into narrow wedges and immediately sprinkle with the lemon juice.

Combine the wine, sugar, cinnamon stick and cloves in a saucepan and slowly bring to the boil. Add the apples and simmer on low heat for 10 minutes. Remove the apples with a slotted spoon and set them aside.

Bring the wine to the boil again and reduce to a thick syrup. Remove the cinnamon stick and cloves. Return the apple wedges to the pan and leave them to cool in the sauce.

Bianco mangiare
Blancmange

3 sheets leaf gelatine
or 1 sachet clear gelatine (7 g/¼ oz)
250 ml/9 fl oz milk
100 g/3½ oz ground almonds
75 g/2½ oz sugar
2 tsp vanilla sugar
1 tsp almond extract
250 ml/9 fl oz double cream

Soak the gelatine in cold water. Combine the milk, almonds and sugar in a saucepan and slowly bring to the boil. Drain or press the liquid from the gelatine. Remove the hot milk from the stovetop and dissolve the gelatine in it, then stir in the vanilla sugar and almond extract. Pour through a sieve into a bowl and leave to cool.

As soon as the mixture starts to become firm, whip the cream and fold it in. Rinse four small soufflé dishes with cold water and fill. Cover them and chill in the refrigerator for at least 3 hours. Before serving, dip the base of each dish briefly into hot water, then turn over on to plates.

Crema di marroni
Sweet Chestnut Mousse

500 g/1 lb 2 oz sweet chestnuts
50 g/1¾ oz sugar
2 tsp vanilla sugar
1 pinch cinnamon
200 ml/7 fl oz double cream
salt
amaretti to garnish

Preheat the oven to 200°C/390°F/gas mark 6. Cut an X into the rounded side of each chestnut, then place them on a baking tray, flat side down, and roast for about 20 minutes until the shells open. Peel the chestnuts and remove the brown membrane.

Put the chestnuts in a saucepan. Add water to cover them and a little salt. Simmer on low heat for about 40 minutes. Drain the chestnuts, then purée in a food processor. Mix in the sugar, vanilla sugar and cinnamon and leave to cool.

Whip the cream and fold it into the cooled chestnut purée. Portion into dessert bowls and garnish with amaretti.

Sweet Chestnuts

There are two types of edible chestnuts: marrons, or *marroni*, and sweet chestnuts, or *castagne*. The true marron is only found in Italy, the Swiss canton of Tessin, and certain regions of France and Spain. Their fruit is somewhat flatter than the common chestnut and is easier to shell. Because of this – and because their flavour is creamier and more intense than that of the common chestnut – they are preferred in the kitchen. At Italian markets, marrons are sold in autumn, fresh from the trees and still in the shell. In supermarkets, one can buy them in cans or jars, already shelled and cooked or puréed.

For centuries, marrons were considered a satisfying staple food – a poor man's potato. Italians said it grew on the *albero del pane*, or 'bread tree'. Due to the chestnut's high starch content, the nuts were ground into flour and used in bread baking. Today, flat loaves of chestnut bread – traditionally baked on hot stones – are sold in Italy as regional specialities. Crystallized or glazed chestnuts are a delicacy enjoyed throughout the country.

Cinnamon

Cinnamon is produced from the bark of thin branches of the evergreen cinnamon tree. The bark is freed of its outer mantel of cork, dried and then cut into pieces. Cinnamon is one of the oldest spices in the world and has its origins in Ceylon, today's Sri Lanka. As has always been the case, the best cinnamon still comes from this island. It is sold as true Ceylon cinnamon, or canela, in sticks or as powder and lends not only desserts, but also meat and vegetable dishes, a distinctive aroma.

Frutti di bosco con gelato
Forest Berries
with Vanilla Ice Cream

250 g/9 oz fresh red currants
250 g/9 oz fresh blackberries
250 g/9 oz fresh blueberries
2 tbsp icing sugar
juice of ½ lemon
juice of 1 orange
60 ml/2 fl oz amaretto
8 slices or scoops vanilla ice cream
fresh mint leaves to decorate

Sort the berries and place them in a bowl. Combine the icing sugar with the lemon and orange juices and amaretto, then pour over the berries. Mix carefully and set aside for 15 minutes.

Place the slices or scoops of ice cream on 4 plates, then top with the berry mixture. Decorate with mint leaves.

Creme caramel
Crème Caramel

250 g/9 oz sugar
1 vanilla pod
300 ml/11 fl oz double cream
300 ml/11 fl oz milk
4 eggs
2 egg yolks

In a small saucepan, heat 150 g/5 oz sugar and 5 tablespoons of water until the sugar caramelizes. Pour the hot caramel into 4 small soufflé dishes and leave to cool. Pre-heat the oven to 150°C/300°F/gas mark 2.

Cut the vanilla pod lengthways and scrape out the seeds. Combine the cream and milk in a clean saucepan, add the vanilla pod and seeds, and slowly bring to the boil. Remove from the heat and take out the vanilla pod.

Beat the eggs and egg yolks with the remaining sugar. Stir in the warm vanilla milk, then pour into the soufflé dishes. Set the soufflés in a baking dish and add enough boiling water in the dish so that the soufflés are two thirds submerged. Place the water bath in the oven for about 40 minutes. Remove the soufflé dishes from the water bath, cool, and chill in the refrigerator overnight to firm.

Before serving, dip the base of each soufflé dish briefly into hot water, then turn over on to dessert plates.

Granita di cachi
Persimmon Granita with Chilli

100 g/3½ oz unsalted pistachio nuts
4 persimmons
1 fresh chilli
100 g/3½ oz sugar
100 ml/3½ fl oz water
juice and grated peel of 1 lemon

Dry-roast the pistachio nuts in a frying pan without added fat, then chop and set aside.

Wash and dry the persimmons and discard the stems. Cut the fruit into small pieces. Halve the chilli lengthways, remove the seeds, and chop finely. Bring the sugar and water to the boil in a small saucepan and cook until the syrup begins to thicken. Cool slightly, then stir in the lemon juice, peel and the chilli.

Purée the fruit and syrup in a food processor. Stir in half the pistachio nuts, then transfer to a metal bowl and place in the freezer. When the mixture begins to harden, use a whisk to stir the frozen fruit from the side of the bowl towards the centre. Continue freezing in this manner until it has a creamy texture. When completely frozen, set the bowl in the refrigerator for 30 minutes to thaw slightly.

Serve portions in champagne glasses with pistachio nuts sprinkled on top.

Sorbetto sprizzetto
Sparkling Sorbet

500 ml/18 fl oz white wine
peel of 1 lemon
175 g/6 oz sugar
juice of 1 orange
100 ml/3½ fl oz Aperol
200 ml/7 fl oz Prosecco
fresh mint leaves to decorate

Combine the wine, lemon peel and sugar in a saucepan and slowly bring to the boil. Simmer 1 to 2 minutes, remove from the stovetop, stir in the orange juice and leave to cool.

Pour the wine syrup through a fine sieve into a bowl and blend in the Aperol liqueur. Pour the mixtue into an ice cream machine and process to sorbet.

Serve the sorbet in long-stemmed cocktail glasses, pour on the Prosecco and garnish with mint leaves.

The Classics

Three famous desserts represent Italian cuisine throughout the world: *tiramisù*, *panna cotta* and *zabaione*. Their international reputation is well established – for many gourmets, without any one of these sinfully creamy delights, a Mediterranean menu is simply incomplete.

Tiramisù (literally, 'pull me up') most likely derives its name from the fact that this perfect mix of espresso, cocoa, sugar and liqueur has an invigorating effect. The original recipe probably has its roots in Tuscany. This dessert's first incarnation was reputedly created in Siena towards the end of the seventeenth century to honour Grand Duke Cosimo III de' Medici. For this famous connoisseur, the confectioners selected only the finest ingredients such as mascarpone made from pure buffalo milk, and perfected their creation with the luxury items chocolate and coffee. The result greatly pleased the grand duke and his female coterie. *Tiramisù* immediately earned a reputation for being not only rich, but also stimulating in every respect.

Panna cotta (literally, 'baked cream') hails from the region of Emilia-Romagna.

This moulded custard numbers among the most delicate temptations northern Italy has to offer, where it is always served with a sauce made of fresh fruit, caramel or chocolate. In other regions, it is also served with marinated fruit.

Zabaione, a light, foamy cream originally made with dry white wine, is a traditional speciality of the Piedmont region. There it is served not only as a dessert, but there is also an unsweetened version that accompanies cooked mixed vegetables. The name of this delicate wine mousse supposedly derives from San Giovanni di Baylon, the patron saint of bakers. The name of its inventor remains just as mysterious as its age. While some sources honour Bartolomeo Scappi, an Italian cook who lived in the sixteenth century, with this distinction, others claim that it made its first appearance in the eighteenth century at the court of Duke Charles Emmanuel of Savoy.

Ingredients for tiramisù *are eggs, mascarpone, sponge fingers, grated chocolate, sugar and espresso.* Tiramisù *can be prepared in a rectangular form (as described in the recipe) or dome-shaped (as shown in the photo below).*

Tiramisù

3 egg yolks
4 tbsp amaretto
150 g/5 oz caster sugar
50 g/1¾ oz plain chocolate, finely grated
500 g/1 lb 2 oz mascarpone
200 ml/7 fl oz double cream
24 sponge fingers
500 ml/18 fl oz strong espresso
cocoa powder for dusting

Whisk together the egg yolks and amaretto. Gradually add the sugar and beat until the sugar has dissolved completely. Stir in the chocolate and mascarpone. Whip the cream and fold it in.

Dip the unsugared side of each sponge finger into the espresso. Arrange half of the sponge fingers on the base of a square or rectangular dish, then cover with half of the mascarpone cream. Layer the remaining sponge fingers and then the cream, spreading it evenly. Cover the dish and chill overnight in the refrigerator. Before serving, dust heavily with cocoa powder.

Fold the mascarpone and whipped cream into the mixture of eggs, sugar and grated chocolate.

Stir amaretto into the resulting cream and put half of it into a piping bag.

Arrange the sponge fingers on a round serving plate and squeeze some of the cream on top.

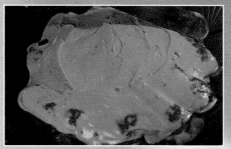

Spread the cream evenly. Repeat in several layers and finish with decorative mounds of cream.

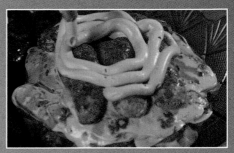

Chill the dessert overnight. Before serving, dust heavily with cocoa powder.

Zabaione

4 egg yolks

4 tbsp sugar

125 ml/4 fl oz Marsala

1 tsp grated lemon peel

Use a whisk to beat the egg yolks, sugar and 1 tablespoon of warm water in a metal bowl until they are thick and very pale.

Place the bowl in a hot water bath and continue to whisk, gradually adding the Marsala. Whisk until the mixture is thick and foamy. Remove the bowl from the water bath, add the lemon peel, and continue to beat until the Zabaione is warm but not hot. Pour into dessert bowls and serve immediately. Zabaione can be served with amaretti or lady finger biscuits, or poured over fresh berries.

For zabaione, whisk the egg yolks with the sugar into a thick, pale cream.

Beat the mixture in a hot water bath until foamy, gradually adding the Marsala.

Panna Cotta

1 vanilla pod

500 ml/18 fl oz double cream

60 g/2 oz sugar

4 sheets or 1½ sachets clear gelatine

500 g/1 lb 2 oz strawberries

3 tbsp icing sugar

Cut the vanilla pod lengthways and scrape out the seeds. In a saucepan, bring the cream to the boil with the pod and seeds. Stir in the sugar. Simmer on low heat for 15 minutes.

Soak the gelatine in cold water for about 10 minutes, then drain or press the liquid from the gelatine. Pour the hot cream through a strainer into a bowl, then dissolve the gelatine in it. Rinse four small soufflé dishes in cold water and fill with the cream. Chill overnight in the refrigerator.

Clean the strawberries, setting aside a few for decoration. Cook the remaining strawberries with the icing sugar. While hot, press the berries through a strainer into a bowl and then leave to cool.

To serve, unmould the soufflé dishes on to dessert plates, top with strawberry sauce and decorate with the reserved whole berries.

Favourite Cakes and Pies

Crostata di limone
Lemon Pie

200 g/7 oz flour	
250 g/9 oz sugar	
5 egg yolks	
grated peel and juice of 2 lemons	
1 pinch salt	
100 g/3½ oz chilled butter	
3 eggs	
150 ml/5 fl oz double cream	
2 tbsp icing sugar	
oil for greasing	

Sift the flour on to a work surface, blend in 100 g/3½ oz sugar and make a well in the centre. Add 4 egg yolks, half the lemon peel, the salt and the butter cut into small pieces. Knead everything into a smooth, supple dough. Form the dough into a ball, cover it in clingfilm and chill for 1 hour in the refrigerator.

Grease a 26-cm/10-inch springform cake tin and preheat the oven to 175°C/350°F/gas mark 4.

On a floured surface, roll out the dough very thin and line the base and sides of the cake tin with it. Use a fork to prick several holes in the dough, then lay a sheet of baking paper over it. Fill the crust with dried beans to prevent buckling and bake for 15 minutes. Remove the dried beans and baking paper and leave the crust to cool.

Reduce the oven temperature to 160°C/320°F/gas mark 3. Beat the remaining egg yolk, the whole eggs and the rest of the sugar and lemon peel into a thick, pale cream. Stir in the lemon juice. Whip the cream and fold it into the egg mixture. Spoon it into the crust and spread it evenly, then bake for 20 minutes. Dust the surface with icing sugar, then return to the oven until golden brown.

Torta di zucca
Pumpkin Cake

175 g/6 oz flour	
125 g/4½ oz butter, plus extra for greasing	
200 g/7 oz sugar	
1 pinch salt	
250 ml/9 fl oz milk	
125 g/4½ oz short-grain rice	
500 g/1 lb 2 oz pumpkin flesh	
2 eggs, whisked	
100 g/3½ oz ricotta	
2 tsp vanilla sugar	
2 tbsp breadcrumbs	
freshly ground pepper	

Sift the flour on to a work surface and make a well in the centre. Add 75 g/2½ oz butter cut in small pieces, half of the sugar, the salt and 75–85 ml/2½–3 fl oz water. Knead everything into a smooth, supple dough. Form the dough into a ball, cover it in clingfilm and chill for 1 hour in the refrigerator.

Combine the milk, 250 ml/9 fl oz water and the rice in a saucepan and bring to the boil. Boil for 2 minutes, then remove from the stovetop and set aside, covered, to cool.

Melt the remaining butter in a second saucepan. Cut the pumpkin flesh into small cubes and cook in the butter until the liquid is absorbed. Purée the pumpkin and stir it into the rice. Stir in the eggs, ricotta, remaining sugar, vanilla sugar and a little pepper.

Grease a 24-cm/9½-inch springform tin and coat the inside of it with the breadcrumbs. Preheat the oven to 200°C/390°F/gas mark 6.

Roll out the dough on a floured surface and line the base and sides of the pan with it. Use a fork to prick several holes in the dough. Spread the rice and pumpkin mixture evenly in the pan and bake 35 to 40 minutes.

Crostata di limone

Crostata di visciole
Cherry Pie

500 g/1 lb 2 oz flour
150 g/5 oz caster sugar
1 pinch salt
2 eggs
grated peel of 1 orange
75 g/2½ oz cold butter
75 g/2½ oz fresh lard
400 g/14 oz sour cherry jam
1 egg yolk, whisked
2 tbsp icing sugar
oil for greasing

Sift the flour on to a work surface, blend in the sugar and make a well in the centre. Add the salt, eggs, orange peel, butter and lard and knead everything into a smooth, supple dough. Form the dough into a ball, cover it in clingfilm and chill for 1 hour in the refrigerator.

Grease a 28-cm/11-inch springform cake tin and preheat the oven to 175°C/350°F/gas mark 4.

On a floured surface, roll out two thirds of the dough very thin and line the base and sides of the pan with it. Spread the jam evenly over the dough.

Roll out the remaining dough and use a pastry wheel to cut it into strips about 2 cm/ ¾ inch wide. Use the strips to form a lattice over the Jam. Brush the top of the pie with the whisked egg yolk, then bake for about 45 minutes.

Leave the pie to cool briefly in the tin, then transfer it to a cooling rack. Before serving, dust with icing sugar.

Picture credits

The publisher would like to thank the following for permission to reproduce copyright material.
All product photographs and cutouts: Martin Kurtenbach, Jürgen Schulzki, Ruprecht Stempell. All other photographs Martin Kurtenbach.

Except the following:
Gunter Beer: all wood backgrounds; 8 (top right & bottom left); 10 (top left & top centre); 11; 12; 13 (except cutout); 16 (steps & large); 17; 18; 20-21(large); 22; 26; 27; 28; 29; 30; 31; 32; 33; 36 (top left); 37; 40; 44; 45; 46; 47; 49; 51; 55; 56; 57; 60; 61; 63; 64; 65; 67; 68; 70; 71; 72; 73; 74; 75; 76; 77; 79 (top right); 83; 84; 86; 87; 88; 89; 94; 95

2 Sandra Ivany/Brand X; 6 Atlantide Phototravel; 8 Botanik Bildarchiv Laux (bottom right); 10 Ruprecht Stempell (top left); 14 Sandro Vannini (top); 15 Sandro Vannini (top); Ruprecht Stempell (steps); 25 Jean-Bernard Vernier (box); 34 Poisson d'Avril/photocuisne; 42 Y. Bagros/photocuisine (top right); Jürgen Schulzki (top right); Sandra Ivany/Brand X (bottom right); 58-59 Jürgen Schulzki; 69 Ruprecht Stempell (top left); 80 Gunter Beer (top left & bottom right)

Front cover: Jürgen Schulzki (beef); Gunter Beer (scampi); Grand Tour (Verona); Gunter Beer (dessert); Grand Tour (Lake Como); Gunter Beer (mullet); Mark Bolton (Venice); Sergio Pitamitz (Tuscany)

Back cover: Gunter Beer